Table of

HARDCORE RESOURCES

Facebook
125,000 followers
Fan: https://www.facebook.com/HardcoreCloser/
Group: https://www.facebook.com/groups/salestalk/
Personal: https://www.facebook.com/realryanstewman

Twitter
10,000 followers
Personal: https://twitter.com/ryanstewman
Business: https://twitter.com/hardcorecloser

LinkedIn
6,000 followers
Personal: https://www.linkedin.com/in/ryanstewman
Business: http://www.linkedin.com/co/hardcorecloser

Instagram
20,000 followers
Personal: https://www.instagram.com/ryanstewman/
Business: https://www.instagram.com/hardcorecloser/

#43 Business Podcast on iTunes, 3,000 subscribers
https://itunes.apple.com/us/podcast/ the-hardcore-closer-podcast/id1098856846?mt=2

YouTube
1.5 million views
https://www.youtube.com/user/ryanstewman

Clyxo
www.Clyxo.com/Closer

Snapchat
ryanstewman

Skype
ryanstewman

Blog
400,000 Visitors Monthly
Sales Talk For Sales Pros
www.HardcoreCloser.com
Articles, Digital Products, Training Resources

Books

- *Bulletproof Business: Protect Yourself Against The Competition (2016)*
- *Kick Ass - Take Names, Emails and Phone Numbers (2015)*
- *Hardcore [c]loser,* ***A Top Business Book of all time, Amazon (Best Seller)*** *(2015)*

PREFACE

Before we get started:

This isn't some rah-rah bullshit book that's designed to make you feel good about having a fucked up life. I wrote this book to show those of you out there who are in the struggle, what's possible if you work for it. Nothing in life is free. Everything costs money or time. Allow me to save you both by reading this book.

Some of the stories you will read in this book will be hard to believe, but they are true nonetheless. I've replayed many of these scenes and scripts in my mind a thousand times, trying to figure out how in the hell things went down the way they did.

At age seven, I was adopted by my stepdad; at age eight, I was put to work by my stepdad; at age 17, I dropped out of school; at age 21, I was in prison; at 23, divorced; at 24, I filed for bankruptcy; at 27, I was in federal prison again; at 28, I was divorced a second time and at 35, divorced a third time.

And that's just the 50,000-foot view. This book will explain how it was all part of a plan from the universe to push me out of my comfort zone and into the hands of **everyday winners** like you. I wrote this book to show those who are oppressed by their past that history doesn't matter if you can develop skills.

The timelines may not be exact, so just go with the flow and enjoy the story. It's about the big picture, not a timeline of when shit happened. Look at each chapter as its own individual story. When it happened is not really as important as the fact that it *did* happen.

Join me, as I share my journey and all of the ups and downs it took me on, with you. Oh, and for protection purposes the names of people have been changed. Also, if you're a cop or government entity, this is all entirely fiction, so chill.

Chapter 1: In The Beginning

You gotta be willing to lose it ALL in order to gain ANY!

Bad news:

In order to get what you want you're going to have to let go of what you don't want.

Even worse news:

You carry around more of what you don't want, than what you want.

The worst news of all: to give up what you don't want means giving up damn near everything. That's right, you must be in a position of being willing to lose it all, before you can have only what you want.

The message you send to the universe, as you carry junk you don't want, is a different message than the one you send when you have only what you want. The longer version is that you send mixed signals to the universe when you ask for one thing, but carry another. You can't ask for peace and have a violent temper. You can't ask for freedom without the willingness to be judged and scolded by those in your circle.

The journey to getting what you want is hard. Even if it is short, it is often painful.

But let me tell you, when you get what you want, and only what you want (taxes excluded) you'll be glad you lost what you did, in order to gain what you have.

*****

One of the fundamentals of being a good fighter is the ability to take an ass whipping. The more you get hit, the more you want to avoid getting hit again. A good fighter is more concerned with defense than offense. Sometimes it only takes one hit to end the fight. No fighter wants to be the one to catch that shot, if it's coming.

You can relate fighting to life. Life is the longest fight you are ever going to enter, and you didn't choose to enter this fight because it was thrown your way. The opponents in this fight are all around you and you never know who, or what, is going to try to kill you next.

In this fight of life, we take risks every day that can kill us. We drive cars, get on planes and take part in all sorts of everyday stuff that can become life threatening in a matter of seconds. Yet, these daily risks are not seen as risky. Even though every day we drive down the highway and see casualties of the road we don't consider driving a risk. Know why? Because we *have* to drive everywhere—it's not a risk, it's a necessity.

Just like the familiarity of driving daily takes away the perceived risk, my familiarity to daily risks increases my drive. All my life I've taken the rocky road, done the wrong thing and learned the hard way. It seems that the "hard way" is the only fucking way I can learn. Hard heads love the hard way.

Childhood

I don't have a lot of fond childhood memories. I'm pretty sure I've mentally repressed most of them due to my adoption at age seven. But what I do remember, I remember vividly.

My family lived in the small town of Leonard, Texas, a typical town that consisted of less than 2,000 people. By family, I mean two sets of grandparents, both parents and several aunts and uncles.

Like any small town, everyone knew each other. This was not always a good or bad thing, but it sure made for fast-spreading gossip. There wasn't shit to do in the town, so people talked a lot—a lot about each other and each other's kids. Nothing special to it, just setting the mood here.

My one grandpa owned the Leonard National Bank and my other grandpa was a full-time entrepreneur who came up with all sorts of amazing ideas in his time. These two guys were the powerhouses in Leonard. They worked together and broke bread together.

It's no coincidence they both had children the same age.

The bank owner's daughter was the hottest chick in town. The entrepreneur's son was a handsome son-of-a-bitch and they were both the same age. All those late night meetings throughout their lives at their parents' places made them the best of friends and eventually lovers.

They were high school sweethearts and as soon as they graduated, they got married and pregnant. All of a sudden it was 1979 and shit got real for the two of them. They created a life together—that life was me. Only one kid, only one chance and here I am.

I was born on October 1, 1979, which means my parents probably had a hell of a New Year's party!

I grew up in Leonard on my grandpa's (the entrepreneur) farm. At the time, my grandpa was a baller. In the 80's his glass factory in Rockwall was slinging shit everywhere. He'd bought each of his four kids a brand new Lincoln and hadn't even flinched when he wrote the check to the dealership that Christmas.

My banker grandpa was a baller, too. Interest rates were so high in the 80's, at 23 percent, that everyone who put money in his bank was winning. If he loaned you cash, you owned him a shit ton more back. I remember my dad telling me he got the hook up from my grandpa at the bank with a 19 percent rate on a car!

I also remember being like three years old and my banker grandpa giving me a one hundred-dollar bill, then my mom took it from me. I didn't know what it was, but I knew it had value because she snatched that shit away as if it were a loaded gun.

Just like anyone else, I've got some quirky-ass family members, too. Especially coming from a small town, on a farm, in Texas. One of those characters is my grandma's brother, Billy. Billy was a goat farmer. Well, I'm not sure that's true…Bill had a lot of goats. We'll just leave it at that.

Maybe he didn't like mowing the yard. I don't know.

So, one day Billy dropped by the house and gave me a goat for my birthday. I was probably four years old at the time because my parents were still together and I wasn't in school yet. Billy dropped the goat off and pulled right out of the driveway leaving my mom fuming hot. In his honor, I named the goat "Billy-Goat." Seemed applicable at the time because it was a male.

When my dad got home, he was pretty entertained at what Uncle Billy had done. My mom convinced my dad to take the goat to the ranch, so he wouldn't be at the house. The ranch was formally known as "The 4 R Ranch," which stood for Ricky, Rachelle, Roxanne and Russell (my dad). Yes. They named all their kids with R's as well as the ranch. I liked it.

My dad was a world champion horse trainer and rider. He's won all sorts of saddles, trophies and been to lots of cool places. He is an entrepreneur in his own right—his right being the animal business.

One day, I accidentally left the gate open that kept Billy, my goat. So, he got in the main barn and ate a good portion of my dad's championship saddle. These saddles are irreplaceable and my dad had a handmade one at the time. Needless to say, he was livid. He gave the goat to the Mexican helper we had, who I'm pretty sure turned it into BBQ. First harsh lesson in life learned.

That next year, I had to start kindergarten. Turned out

Uncle Billy's wife, my aunt, was the principal at the

Leonard Elementary School. My mom worked at the time and my dad traveled a lot, so I would get dropped off at my great grandma's house, who lived right by the school. I would walk to school, even in kindergarten.

The very first day in school I got my ass kicked. My aunt, the principal, decided to instill corporal punishment on me. I'm sure I deserved it. After all, it was family and all, but I don't remember what I did. I just remember the punishment.

From the moment that happened on day one of school, I knew I hated school and didn't want to be there. There were too many rules when I was young and as I got older most of it sounded like BS. The teachers all knew I hated school, too. I must have had some crazy shit written in my folder. I would lash out often and teachers hated when I did so. But I only did it because they hated it!

When I was six, my parents split up and my mom briefly moved to Allen, Texas, a town about 40 minutes from Leonard with a population of approximately 30,000 people. It's considered a suburb of Dallas. I completed the first grade there and school was a little cooler in the city, but it still sucked.

While we may have lived in Allen, my mom couldn't escape Leonard. She fell in love with a long-haired, skinny dude named Keith who would later adopt me to relieve my dad of the back child support he owed. This all happened when I was in the second grade.

Keith adopted me and my last name changed. I was so angry at my dad for letting this happen that I changed my middle name, too. I was born Ryan Russell McCord and I'm now Ryan Keith Stewman.

Can you imagine going back to the place you hate, school, and now having to explain to everyone why your whole fucking name is different? The kids made fun of me because they didn't understand. Hell, I didn't understand. It was a fucked deal no one was happy about.

While I had hated school for the teachers at first, when I returned after my adoption, I hated the kids, too. I couldn't wait to get the fuck out. As I got older, I found plenty of ways to avoid or skip as much of it as I could.

Chapter 2: School? Fuck School!

If you ever hear me say "I'm not smart" after I tell you these stories, you will know exactly why I say it. Growing up in the 90's was weird. It was a time of gangster rap and death metal. Everyone wanted to be a tough guy. High school seemed like prison at times. I hated conflict and school, so I usually didn't attend any classes.

I remember showing up to first period one time and my teacher asking me who I was. I had gotten in a fight with one of the crew I skipped school with and wanted to make a change. When I decided to go to class and my teacher didn't know me, I realized just how far behind I'd gotten in attendance.

One day, around 12:45 in the afternoon the tension was hot in our school. Someone had been pulling the fire alarm once or twice a day. These instances were almost always blamed on me. I'm here to tell you, I never once pulled a fire alarm in my life. The "authority figures" didn't believe me.

I showed up to the lunchroom and the students started yelling at me for pulling the alarm. I explained to them that it wasn't me. They insisted, much like my teachers, that it was, and my shenanigans were distracting them from getting an education.

One particular chick felt compelled enough to call me names to the point I had to tell her, "Bitch shut the fuck up, I told you it wasn't fucking me. So lay the fuck off me!" I still remember the look on that pretty bitch's face. She'd never been talked to like that before, especially by a dude. Everyone kissed her ass and wanted to fuck her, so no one had ever requested that she shut the fuck up.

In the middle of the lunchroom, with noises at an all-time high, this screaming conversation is taking place between me and this bitch's crew. Now, I was not popular in high school and I didn't want to be, I wanted to get the fuck out of there.

After the screaming subsided, I noticed a few of the girls in the crowd had their boyfriends with them. One of the boyfriends was this muscular dude who all the ladies in our school had a crush on. This dude, Peter, had a thing for the chick I'd told to "shut the fuck up" in a major way. I didn't hang out with any of these people, so I was not privy to the hierarchy of who was crushing on whom.

Apparently, the chick was so upset at what I said to her, she petitioned this Peter guy to beat my ass.

After the next class period, as I was walking down the hall minding my own business, Peter came up behind me and tapped my shoulder. When I turned around to see who tapped, he punched me right in my face and took off. I remember asking my homeboy who was walking with me, "What happened? Did I run into the pole in the middle of the hall?" He laughed and said, "Fool, Peter just knocked you out!" This shit hurt my pride more than it hurt my face.

I wasn't about to let this fucker get away with that shit.

I had some passes to get kids out of class that I carried on me. I would forge them from time-to-time, in order to get my boys out of class when I needed to. One of my friends went with me as we looked in every class window in the school trying to find the room Peter was in.

When we spotted him, I quickly filled out the pass sheet and knocked on the door.

The teacher answered: "How can I help you?"

Me: "I'm here from the office and have a pass sheet for Peter."

Teacher: "Okay, let me get him and send him with you."

She had no clue what was about to transpire. Peter got up looking like a big shot. Like I had told on him and he was about to get in trouble. Actually, it was quite the contrary. I've never been one to tell authorities shit. I am an antiauthoritarian and always have been.

As soon as the door closed and the teacher had her back turned, I punched Peter in the face. I expected him to be tougher, but that wasn't the case. He fell into the door and made a loud sound. The teacher came running over then got on the CB to call the school police and principal.

While we waited on everyone to arrive and save Peter, I continued to beat the shit out of his head with my feet. I was beating him for more reasons than I knew at the time.

I had to let it all out. I fucked Peter up. Bad.

Funny how things worked out. As I went to get Peter out of class to go to the principal's office, that's exactly where both of us wound up. Peter got a two-day suspension and I got kicked out of school. It felt unfair, but fuck it, I didn't want to go to school anyways.

My parents didn't want the responsibility of keeping up with me since I was not in school, so they begged the school to put me in isolation. Which eventually, to keep graduate numbers up, the school obliged. I ended up for about two weeks in this room all alone. I was so far away from everyone in school, I managed to trip on LSD two days in a row and no one even noticed. I was not bored while I was there!

Back before the interwebs, chicks would pass notes instead of texting. I got a note from one of the cheerleaders who happened to be in Peter's class that day saying she thought I was cute and she wanted me to come to the pep rally and see her after.

This chick was hot, so of course I was gonna go!

When I showed up at school for the pep rally, I ran into the principal. This Dr. Troxell guy was a clown. He ran the school like the military. In Plano, the city next door, kids had open lunch and could have long hair, earrings and whatever, as long as they got good grades. In Allen, with Troxell, he wanted only clean cut, no earring-wearing Mormon look-alikes in attendance. At the time, Allen's population was about 60 percent rich-ass Mormons.

Needless to say, I wasn't their ideal citizen or student.

Troxell came up to me and with his coffee-stained teeth and shit-smelling breath said, "Boy, if you want to set foot in my school, you better take them earrings out." I replied, "It's after school and I'm not even a student here anymore.

I think I'll be okay, Trox."

His face turned beet red and you could see his eyes creating steam from the saline in them. He was livid. He'd probably never been talked back to in his life. But fuck it. What did I have to be scared of? With a stepdad that could squat 800 pounds, and who hit me on the regular, I wasn't scared of this pussy.

Troxell said, "Boy, I'm not playing with you, you better get off school grounds," and he pushed me with his fingertips.

I lost my fucking mind. My testosterone levels were so high all I could do was think about hitting him in his face. Instead, I pushed him back. The motherfucker went Vietnam on me! He called the cops, and even the damn newspaper. I was arrested and taken to the City of Allen jail. My first of many visits.

I was fully expelled from school that day and never returned. I've had dreams about going back, but they were more like nightmares. Two days later, I turned 17 and took my GED exam. I passed it and went into the real world, the place I'd always wanted to live anyway.

Chapter 3: Working at the Car Wash

When I was about eight, my stepdad decided he'd had enough of my ADD and put me to work at the car wash he managed.

At first, I mowed the yards. He'd pick me up after school and on the weekends and put me to work mowing. It was actually good business sense on his end. He got cheap labor to mow yards at his five locations and he got to occupy me so he wouldn't be worried about me causing trouble, while I got to learn the value of earning a dollar.

My stepdad quickly recognized the hard work gene in me. It wasn't long before I was not only mowing the yards, I was also starting to vacuum cars as they came in. As I got faster and faster at vacuuming, my stepdad would pick me up more often to go to work.

At 10 years old, I felt what it was like to be in college. I went to school full-time and worked 15-20 hours a week part time at the car wash. It sucked. I had no friends other than the neighborhood kids and the Mexicans at work.

Obviously, I didn't speak Spanish, so I had no clue what the dudes at the car wash were saying. I just worked. Most days, I was the only white dude on the job. Even more than that, I was the only one on the job who spoke English.

I soon fixed the language barrier by learning Spanish. It was the only seventh grade class I'd paid attention in. I didn't pass it, but I got what I needed out of it. The rest of my Spanish speaking talent came from the guys at the car wash who helped me further my vernacular. Turns out being bilingual was a major plus. By the time I was 13, I was a service advisor. That meant minimum labor, but maximizing sales for the car wash.

My job was to convince customers to buy the more expensive packages. Say someone comes in and wants a $10 car wash and we have washes from $10 to $40. My job was to sell the higher packages.

After coming up and doing all the jobs on the car wash assembly line, I had a vast knowledge of how the whole operation worked. That knowledge meant sales power! My average ticket price per car was usually around $16.50. Which means, if we washed a thousand cars in 10 hours it was $16,500 in earnings for the day.

Needless to say they loved me in the sales job. One of the managers gave me a set of Zig Ziglar tapes when I was about 14 and they changed the way I sold shit. I was a legend at age 16 in the car business. One day, I wrote tickets for over 1,600 cars in 10 hours.

When one of the mangers got wind of how much my commission checks were from someone in the corporate office, he was livid that my check was almost twice as much as his. He raised such a big ruckus that they took his commission side of the pay structure away shortly after.

This was my very first experience with management hating sales guys because we make "too much."

When I was around 15, I was working in the front of the car wash helping put tire dressing on the cars as they came out of the tunnel. It was a particularly hot and busy day. Being the young dude who was shorter than most, yes even the Mexicans, it was my job after school that day to do the bitch job.

About two hours into dressing several hundred tires, my stepdad showed up with a major chip on his shoulder. I don't know if his boss had yelled at him or what, but I could see the look of anger in his eyes.

He started nit picking me on how to dress tires. After several minutes of annoying the fuck out of me, I told him, "I've never even seen you dress a tire. What the fuck do you know? Can you even bend over this far to do it? If not, please just let me do my thing."

He was fucking livid! He dragged me in front of the customers and everyone else out back and beat the shit out of me. When I tried to fight back he put my 15-year old, 130-pound body into a chokehold and damn near killed me. The capillaries busted in my eye.

When we got home that night, he and my mom fought for obvious reasons and I was told I was not allowed to go back to work at the car wash… at least for a while.

My uncle ran an electrical company and they were always hiring people to pull wire through the custom homes they'd contracted. After some begging, he reluctantly hired me.

I thought I hated the car wash job, but I for sure, hated being an electrician because of the heat. It's so fucking hot in Texas attics in the summer.

Since I had a busted capillary in my eye, everyone always looked at me funny. Little did I know at 15 years old, my fucked up eye was a sign of a meth addiction. See, apparently when you do meth and stay up all night, your eyes bust due to stress and lack of sleep.

I had no clue about this and never thought of it, but the other workers did. They would always offer me meth, cocaine and weed. I never did meth or cocaine, but I had smoked weed a few times in my life and loved it.

I had buddies who sold weed and I could tell these old dudes loved buying the shit and selling it to their homeboys. I saw an opportunity there real quick and got in touch with one of the older kids from the neighborhood. Then I bought weed from him with my paycheck. It was like a half pound for $250. Yes, weed was that cheap in my day.

I'd sell ounces for $65 to these dudes all day long. They made me more money from selling weed than I made from working. I'd front these fuckers on a Monday and take their whole checks on Friday. It was nuts.

Until one day, when I got cut on a heating unit in an attic and had to go to the ER. When I got there, they gave me a drug test for weed, which I failed. My uncle had to fire me. My parents were enraged and my mom blamed me for getting all those guys on drugs.

My stepdad had no choice but to hire me back at the car wash. This time though, he made me work at the Dallas location. It was a way busier store and they needed a fast service advisor to keep up. I was the guy.

I grew up in the country and in the suburbs. I was not familiar with urban life and the car wash was right by one of Dallas' most notorious drug neighborhoods. I had no clue the dudes who came in to get their fancy cars washed, who wore all that gold, were drug dealers. I thought they were doctors or some shit.

One day, one of the regulars asked me if I smoked weed. I told him, "Of course!" and he gave me a free quarter bag as a tip. I asked if he could get more and he gave me his beeper number along with a code for me to use.

I still remember beeping him on December 31, 1997 and asking him, "C-Pain can you get bit weight? You know like

a quarter pound of weed?" He laughed and said, "You think that's a lot? Don't worry lil' nigga, I got ya."

I was paying around $200 a quarter pound from the neighborhood guy and C-Pain was gonna sell them to me

for $125. Before you could blink, I became the neighborhood weed man. The smokers loved me.

Turned out C-Pain sold more than weed and I was about to learn that side of the business.

Chapter 4: Let's Do Some Gangster Shit

C-Pain and I had a love-hate relationship. He loved the money I paid him, but hated me.

I had no clue how "the game" worked. All I knew was that I had grown up accustomed to giving top-notch service to clients and he obviously hadn't.

Imagine the scene:

When I met C-Pain, I was a 16-year old, scrawny white kid with long blonde hair from the suburbs, and he was a 30+ year old muscular black dude, who had not only killed people when he was in the military in Iraq, but he'd killed quite a few in the hood, too. Motherfuckers were scared to death of C-Pain, but I was too stupid to understand the magnitude of the situation. I kept a zero-balance business relationship with him for three years.

When I was about 18 or 19, my stepdad fired me from the car wash and kicked me out of the house...again. I had no way to get money, so I needed C-Pain's help in a bad way.

But first let me tell you the reason I got fired. It's quite a story.

I was working as the service advisor at the car wash in Dallas. The same one I'd met C-Pain in. There was a rule at the car wash. Due to it usually being an all-male staff, they did not hire good looking chicks as cashiers. This kept the guys who were on break from lingering around the cashier's desk on slow days.

Well, one summer the rule got broken and they hired this 19-year old blonde girl named Lauren. As a hormone driven youngster with only one chick around day-in-and day-out, I started to develop feelings for the girl. The feeling that I wanted to fuck her really bad!

But, alas, I was not the only one who felt this way. The manager, Larry, who was about 28 at the time, also had a hard on for the hot cashier. Not to mention all the other dudes who weren't even allowed inside. Hell, I'm guessing my stepdad wanted to fuck her, too. That must've been how she got hired!

Anyways, I ended up sealing the deal in my living room one night. I never told anyone, but everyone knew, including Larry. Larry had everything I didn't. He was 6' 4", 250 pounds and muscled. He probably also had a huge cock and made way more money than me.

It wasn't too long after Lauren and I had started "going out" that I became insanely jealous of Larry. Especially since I had to go to school during the week and they were alone.

On rainy days when the car wash closed early, it would drive me nuts. This was before cell phones, when we used beepers and home phones.

One day, Lauren tells me she cheated on me with Larry during an argument we were having. I was livid.

I got home later that afternoon to find Larry and my stepdad chillin' at the house. I confronted Larry and instead of minding his business or taking my side, my stepdad defended Larry. I felt like I didn't have anyone on my team. I was clearly in the right, while father of the year over here was on my ass.

So, I told my stepdad to fuck off and pushed him out of my face. He swung at me and missed. I could hear the whoosh his big-ass fist made as it swished by my ear. I ran upstairs, but he caught me about three stairs up and jumped on top of me.

I had no choice but to kick him in the nuts. He had already choked me to the point of my eyes bursting a few months back, now he was going to break my face in. I kneed him in the nads with every ounce of power I could and slid right out from under him, before basically hovering up the remaining stairs to my room.

Turns out the lock and the door in my bedroom were not stepdad proof. He busted through them like one of those tackling dummies defensive linemen hit in football practice. I knew he was gonna kill me, so I made a quick decision to jump out of the window. I dropped from high up on the second story straight onto my right hand and broke it.

I ran away from home and didn't call or anything for months. I also didn't have a job or any money to get my right hand fixed, which sucks because I'm right handed.

Now that you understand the situation, and how I needed money in a bad way at 17 years old, you'll have some sort of empathy for the situations I was in that I'm about to share with you.

I had a long-time homeboy named Brant who had a dad and a brother who lived in the next town over. Somehow, I convinced Brant's dad to let me live with him rent-free. Brant's dad was an easy-going stoner, but he had a wife at the time who was crazy.

I'd wake up at 4am to them screaming at each other as I tossed around on the floor in Brant's brother's room. It was just a fucked living situation altogether. Worst part, I only had one set of clothes. Yep, that's right, only one pair of underwear!

I had to hustle some money up quick. The year was 1997. The only reason I remember this is because I had bought a brand new 1997 Chevy S-10 truck to drive, but my mom had co-signed and taken it away, despite the fact that I still made the monthly payment on it.

I had to get a vehicle, clothes and a place to live. Only way I knew how to make money fast was by selling dope. So, that's exactly what the fuck I did.

I've met rich kids who sell drugs and I've always despised them. Selling drugs is a grimy-ass job and people who think it's cool to idolize or emulate drug dealers are fucked up. They have no clue the struggle. You may be reading this thinking *dude, selling drugs is easy*. And you're right, but collecting money and dealing with the people you have to deal with are not easy.

I didn't have the luxury of selling drugs to rich kids. I didn't know anyone, but poor-ass car wash workers, electricians and gangsters. I had no idea how much chaos would enter my life in such a short amount of time.

I convinced Brant's brother to take a job with me at a car wash in Dallas. He had a vehicle and needed a job. I got both of us hired based on my skills and he agreed to drive us to work each day. In the car wash business, Saturdays may bring in 1,000+ cars to be washed. When it's 112 degrees outside and hard hot work is involved, most people drop out.

That was one of my first life lessons. When the work shows up, most people will refuse to do it. That's exactly what Brant's brother did after about two hours. He quit. He was my only ride, so it forced me to quit, too. I was fucking embarrassed to say the least.

We left the car wash and went directly to some trailer park in Wylie, Texas to this white trash dude's silver bullet. Soon as we got in, Brant's brother and this trashy-ass dude put some powder up their nose. I asked what it was and they told me "crank." Like a moron, I asked if I could have some.

I guess I was hoping to relieve the stress from quitting that job. I'm not a quitter and it kills me to do so. I sniffed the peanut butter brown, melty substance they had lined out on the sink.

It burned with the absolute fucking worst pain my nose had ever experienced. I remember immediately turning around and asking, "Is it supposed to burn like this?" Of course, they told me it was and then said something like, "You gotta burn to earn." About an hour later, the drug finally quit hurting and kicked in.

I remember feeling good for a few hours and then crashing hard. That was the last time me and hard drugs would go around for a while.

During that drug-induced experience, I had a realization. I didn't like crank or the high it gave me, but there was obviously a huge demand for it. Unlike weed, which I loved so much I was known to smoke up my margins.

I knew I could sell crank, and make money. So, I beeped C-Pain and told him I was coming over to re-up. When I arrived at his apartment off Skillman Street in Dallas, I proposed my business model to him.

There were three to four other black dudes in his apartment listening to 17-year old me, give a Shark Tank-style pitch on why I wanted to sell crank to white folks. C-Pain, after laughing his ass off and refusing to share the blunt with me, said, "Man, I fucked with that crank shit once. You remember that (insert other black dude's nickname)? Remember that nigga, Reggie? Yeah, I had to shoot him and his brother behind that shit. I'll never fuck wit' it again and I suggest you do the same, white boy."

Well fuck...

I didn't like being turned down, but I also wasn't willing to shoot at motherfuckers over drugs. C-Pain then offered up a solution to my problem.

"Hey man, you ever do coke? I mean you said you did crank and didn't like it; you can't keep your shit together with weed. Ever think about selling coke? I only charge $500 for a BIG O and you could sell eight balls for $180 each. Since you don't do the shit, you could make $890 profit on every $550 invested."

My ears were wide open and receptive as fuck to his proposal. I'd seen a lot of the white kids in school snort coke, so fuck it, I gave it a shot. I bought two pounds of weed and an ounce of coke with money I had raised from Brant's brother and his friends. They were about to be in for a treat when I got back.

I don't remember whose car I borrowed to get to C-Pain's place, but they were pissed when I got back. One thing about C. was that he didn't like you to run in and out of his house. You might have to chill with him for a couple hours. It didn't bother me because I enjoyed his street wisdom and deep stoner talks, but the person waiting on me, who'd given me their money, hated the wait. Druggies are so impatient.

When I returned, I sold all of the weed and then all of the eight balls for $150. Literally, I had pushed everything in about five minutes. All of a sudden I had about $1,000 cash. That shit changed the game for me in a major way.

After repeating this process a few times, I started to miss home. The day-in-and-day-out drug buyers drove me nuts. I needed "love" and structure in my life, so I called Mom and asked to come home.

To say my folks were suspicious as hell when I arrived home was an understatement. I had no job, yet I had new clothes and even a nice, new fat necklace. I told them I bought it with my car wash check, but my stepdad ran car washes, he knew how much new hires made. When he called the place where I'd told him I worked (because he knew the manager there), the manager told him I'd only worked two hours and that was weeks ago.

My stepdad came home, found some weed in my room and kicked me back out. No truck, no clothes...just gone.

I walked up the street to my boy Chilly Willy's apartment. He lived there with Beth, his girl and their kid. Chilly Willy was a weird-ass dude but he was willing to let me crash as long as I gave him a little coke. Seemed like a good deal at the time.

Chilly Willy's coke addiction got rough quick and he started running up a tab with me. Before long, it was like $600 and he had no way to pay. He offered me to fuck his old lady, but she was no $600 lay.

I needed that money because C-Pain wouldn't let me not pay him, so I had to make a rough decision. I was gonna have to fuck Willy up and take his shit, then sell it to get my money.

I'd known Chill Will for a decade and I couldn't bring myself to do it. So, I paid two of my homies to kick his door in and demand the cash or take his shit. I sat out front in the car and waited. I asked them not to hurt his wife, but Willy was open game.

They kicked the door in, pushed Will on the floor and low and behold that fucker came up with $600 cash immediately. I knew it was all he had from his paycheck and his kid would be hungry, but that wasn't the case after all. Turned out he had family who could help him.

My boys grabbed my shit on the way out and even though I had my money and clothes, I was homeless and car-less again.

Chapter 5: Let's Get Stupid and Reckless

One day, I walked over to Brant's house before he had to leave for school. To my surprise, my good homeboy, Shad was over there with a brand new Mercury Cougar. Shad was a great guy, not a trouble maker. Everyone, including me, loved him dearly.

Shad, Brant and I used to smoke weed, trip acid and talk about life on a regular basis. We shared millions of laughs and stories that could fill ten books. The three of us were best friends for about a three-year period.

So, back at Brant's house, Shad has this badass new car. I asked jokingly, "Dude, where the fuck did you steal that from?" He said, "It's not stolen dude. Chris' mom is out of town and she left it with him. He owes me like $100, so he let me use it. Let's drive it to California and party our asses off!"

Shad, Brant, a guy named Brett (RIP) and I were all in a garage band. We played the fuck out of some punk rock shit. We used to get high as giraffe pussy and jam like a mug! Shad figured a punk rock band had a better chance in Cali than it did in Texas.

I've always been a quick decision maker, so I jumped in the car with $50, one set of underwear, two joints and exuberant expectations. We didn't even have a map. Shad just knew we needed to go west and that's what we did.

Hopped in the car and pointed it west.

Since we had no map, we went the worst way ever. About three hours into West Texas we needed gas and food. We also had the munchies from one of the two joints we'd smoked earlier.

We rolled up to some Podunk gas station in the middle of nowhere. Shad took the front of the car and pushed the vending machine in front of the doorway, so the clerk couldn't get out. This was way before auto pumps and credit card prepays. Back then, you got gas then walked in and paid for it. Even the gas shut off switches had to be outside for EPA purposes.

So, this poor clerk is stuck inside watching as we take all the chips off the racks, pack all the sodas and beer into the trunk and fill our car up with premium. After all, that's what it said to use on the gas tank.

The one smart thing I did, was switch license plates from Brant's car to the Cougar. I didn't tell Brant or Shad I had done it. I wasn't 100 percent sure we had permission to use the car, so I figured that would be safe.

I imagine as the clerk called in a license plate number, the cops looked for a red Tempo, not a silver Cougar. We were winning!

Speaking of winning, we now had munchies and a shit ton of beer from that lick we'd just pulled off. We were now set for at least the duration of the ride in Texas.

I don't know if you realize it or not, but it's further from Dallas to El Paso than it is from El Paso to Los Angeles. In other words, it's a long-ass boring drive through West Texas. The beer definitely helped to pass the boredom.

Right before we crossed the Texas/New Mexico border, we hit one more lick similar to the last one, but this time we got more shit and mid-grade gas. They didn't carry premium.

Once we got about 100 miles into New Mexico, it was about 11pm Texas time. When we pulled over to piss at a store, I hopped on the payphone and called my mom, telling her, "Mom, I'll be out of town for a few days. Don't worry about me, okay?" I was drunk and I guess I missed my mom.

This was right during the time when caller ID had first come out. My mom recognized that the number was from a payphone in New Mexico and called the cops. I guess in her mind, she thought I was leaving her for good. It was one thing for me to be homeless running around nearby somewhere, but it was another if I left the state.

I guess the cops traced the call and put an APB out. Not for the stolen car or anything...but for me. They were smart enough to figure we were traveling west on the highway we were on, so the APB was to look out for three teens in a car with Texas plates.

As we rolled into Tula Rosa, New Mexico a cop followed us. I was laying down in the backseat, trying to stop the world from spinning, so I didn't know he was there. Shad said, "Shit! It's a cop!" and I rose up and looked out the back window.

As soon as the cop saw me, and counted three people in the car, he flashed the cherries. Shad wanted to make a run for it, but I talked him out of it. He reluctantly pulled over and the cop walked up to us, gun drawn. I guess my bitch of a mom probably told them I was a drug dealer or whatever. She was evil to me like that.

He instructed all three of us to exit the car and he asked for IDs, saying, "You know, I almost didn't pull you guys over, but when the third one there got up to look out the window, I knew it was you guys on the APB."

Shad immediately said, "Ryan, you're a fucking retard," and hit me. I deserved it. I had called my mom, and I had now gotten us pulled over. This was it, jail again, but this time in a whole new state.

The cop cuffed and searched us, then called for another car to help him transport us. Once we got to the police station, we realized there was not a jail, just an office. They took off the handcuffs, told us we were not under arrest, but detained until our parents could come get us. We were left to sleep in the chief of police's office.

While there, I dyed my hair red in the sink. That pissed them off pretty good. The head cop said, "That's a dipshit move to make. You guys got a lot of growing up to do. If you'd have got arrested one city over, you'd be getting ass raped by Indians." Funny thing, I still didn't realize how fucking stupid I was. I kept making dumb shit moves and I don't know why.

If that wasn't enough, we still had to call our parents and ask them to come one state over and personally get us.

FML

After we made the calls and took the ass chewings, the parents elected to send my stepdad to pick up all three of us. I assumed they'd paid my dad's plane ticket since it was 4-6 hours later before he could get us out.

After the call, I realized I still had that other joint! So Shad, Brant and my redheaded dumb-ass walked over to the park and smoked that bad boy. We reflected on how fucking stupid I was and the shit I got all three of us into. It still didn't sink in, though.

When my stepdad arrived to get us, he brought one of the car wash managers, Andrew (RIP) with him. Andrew was from the next town over and his dad was head jailer in the same city the cop had warned us about.

My stepdad brought him as a companion, and as someone who knew their way around. They rented a SUV, which was a new thing at the time, and after they got us from jail, my stepdad took Andrew to visit his grandma. Come to think about it, and especially since Andrew died a few years later, it was a nice gesture on my stepdad's end.

After my stepdad had said his initial two cents, we three were instructed to not say a fucking word until we were all in our own homes back in Texas. He wasn't trying to hear shit. He and Andrew got on the plane with the three of us and started drinking their asses off.

When I got home my stepdad didn't beat me. He didn't yell. He simply told me I now owed him $1,500 for plane tickets, food, his time, the car rental and everything else.

He ended it with, "Congratulations, you got your job back at the car wash and now you work for Andrew as his bitch."

To make matters worse, the car was stolen. When Chris's mom got back she filed charges on all three of us. My bills kept piling up.

I hired a lawyer and he got the charges dropped, but Shad and Brant were both charged with UUMV as minors and the two of them were not to see each other until their 18th birthdays. Little did we three know that Shad would die on Brant's 18th birthday…but that's for later in the book.

Chapter 6: Paying the Dues

Andrew managed the car wash in Dallas, the one where I'd met C-Pain. So, this was the most convenient job for me to have at the time.

C-Pain had a couple of different cool rides, so he was in the car wash often. When he came in to get his shit washed, he'd stop off in the parking garage below and put weed and coke in my Jeep for me. I'd leave my Jeep unlocked and the cash in a bank bag he had the key for.

Andrew could tell C-Pain and I were up to something. He was no idiot; Andrew was extremely street smart. He always seemed one step ahead of any of my shenanigans.

I always had the feeling like Andrew smoked weed. I'd offered him free shit, but he always said, "No." Even a few of the car wash workers who bought from me mentioned they had gotten high with Andrew. He must have respected my stepdad enough not to get high with me.

He was the only one, though. Throughout my tenure at the car wash I bet I got high with 20 different managers.

One day, I needed some weed for a client and C-Pain couldn't make it to the car wash. He gave me an address and told me to meet him at his apartment.

At this time in my life, the term "trap house" wasn't a thing. Well, it was a thing, just not a phrase people used to describe locations with narcotics. We simply called them "dope spots."

This was definitely a dope spot. I was really naive at the time, but in retrospect, I'm 100 percent sure C-Pain didn't live in this apartment. Even though another guy he'd met through me at the car wash, Reggie (RIP), was his "roommate."

What was really going on was that Reggie lived in a dope spot and C-Pain took care of the rent.

When I showed up at the apartment for the first time, C-Pain had about 10 trash bags full of pounds of weed and a good half key of coke laid out on the table. Reggie was sitting in a recliner smoking a king-sized blunt with the car wash shoe shine guy, Ray.

Fuck. I had no idea C-Pain hung out, lived, or sold to anyone else in the car wash. At that moment, I realized how good he was at keeping a secret.

I hadn't been over at "Reggie's dope spot" for 15 minutes when there was a knock on the door. The spot was on the third floor, so we had heard someone coming up the stairs.

When Reggie answered the door, it was Andrew! Andrew was apparently a stoner. He was there to pick up some weed on the way home. Reggie welcomed him in like this was a pretty normal occurrence. But when Andrew walked in the kitchen and saw my 17-year old ass smoking a blunt with the drug king of Dallas, the look in his eye was pure rage.

He said all of three words to me, pulled C. off to the side and was gone in less than five minutes. I asked C-Pain, "Why the fuck you let him leave in five minutes and I gotta stick around for an hour each time?" He said, "'Cause I don't like that motherfucker. He's shady as hell. Don't trust him."

In hindsight, Andrew probably told C-Pain to stop fucking with me, and C-Pain didn't want some car wash Mexican telling him how to make his money. That's not what was in my 17-year old mind, though. I just thought Andrew was shady. Turns out he was the opposite of that.

Eventually, I would pay my stepdad back everything I owed him from working for the car wash. I had used my drug earnings to go out, buy clothes and other shit. It wasn't a bad spot for a 17-year old to be in.

Until it ended.

Then one day, something happened. Andrew and I got into it and he fired me. My stepdad kicked me out of the house again and I was homeless. It was about a month before I turned 18, so even with a job, no apartment would rent me a place.

I crashed on Chilly Willy's couch and a few others, too. I mainly sold drugs, but I had gained employment at a place called Central Electric, which was within walking distance from one of the couches where I'd crashed.

There was this chick, Jenn. She was 23, and her husband was in the brig in the Army for some shit. She was lonely, needed dick and had a place for me to stay.

Believe it or not, I've got a good conscience. While it was nice to have go-to pussy, I also felt guilty for fucking a married ho. But, she was close to the electric house and it just seemed to work out. Her mom lived there, too and never questioned shit. Quality people, you know....

The day Brant turned 18, he and I went over to Shad's house to all reunite, smoke a blunt and kick it like old pals again. Brant picked me up from Jenn's house that Saturday and we rode to Plano to tell Shad we were getting an apartment together and to come help us move.

Apparently, Shad had partied with the brown lady the night before. I knew heroine was a big deal in the suburbs, but I had never seen it and I damn sure hadn't known Shad was into it.

When Brant and I walked through that front door, Shad was on the couch, purple as fuck. Dead as shit. I don't know if I cried or what; it all happened so fast. I also don't remember if it was me or Brant who had to break the news to his folks who were asleep in the master bedroom.

What a fucked day that was. There were so many lessons to be learned and I ignored them all. I'd just lost one of my best friends. The first and only friend I'd ever had die on me and I still kept the hustle.

I was so far gone into the game. I went to the funeral and then did my best to forget Shad had ever existed. That's just my way of dealing with pain.

At the funeral, I ran into a dude named Nathan I used to see around. He and this dipshit, Francis were always palling around like butt buddies and I didn't trust either of them.

Nathan hit me up and said, "Hey man, Shad told me you got the hook up on weed and blow. Is this true?" I should have told him to fuck off, but I needed the money and the hustler inside me just wanted to charge him extra, so I gave him my beeper number.

Within a few days of Brant turning 18, we had an apartment in Plano, Texas. We were the first ones to live in the brand new unit. Neither of us had a car, but I got Brant a job at Central Electric and it was only a five-minute walk to and from work each day.

We got dishes, furniture and the like, little-by-little. We both worked during the day and I sold drugs at night. Brant never sold drugs, he just used them.

One of the regulars who would stop by was Nathan. Nathan had a car, so I used him to give me rides to C-Pain's house. Since I wasn't in Dallas or at the car wash any more, C-Pain was a way's away. C. hated the suburbs and refused to deliver.

When Nathan would take me to his house, C. would make Nathan wait in the car, sometimes for as long as two hours. Nate hated that shit. Always bitched at me like I could do something about it.

One day, Nathan showed up to take me to re-up and I was drunk. When we got to C-Pain's house,

Nathan convinced me to introduce him. I took Nathan up to the door with me.

C-Pain flipped the fuck out. It was bad enough that one dumb-ass white boy from the suburbs was in his business, let alone two. He was livid. I bet if I wasn't white, he would have killed me and dumped my body.

Nate was not to be trusted either. He somehow got C-Pain's number from my phone and beeped him with my code. When the page was returned, he told C. I'd given him his number. All without my knowledge. That shady fucker.

The next time I saw C-Pain, he damned near killed me. I told myself I was done with him and the dope gang.

That didn't mean I didn't have bills to pay; I was just tired of dealing with C. and all the drama. Cocaine was a whole different game than weed and it wasn't played by the rules.

So, I made one last trip to C-Pain's to pick up my biggest load ever. I still remember the day. It was Jan 19, 1999. I had been fired from my job, my girlfriend of two years had dumped me and I was leaving the dope game all at the same time. What a fucking rock bottom it was (or so I thought).

After I got in from C-Pain's, I immediately sold the whole haul minus about seven grams. Brant, (still my roommate) decided to take a few to the head. I'd given him some for free, he was my homie for life, so I never charged him. He didn't do it very often, though.

After a few hours of sitting in my misery, Brant said, "Hey man, you look like shit. Let's get on the papers and call a couple hookers. You can put it on my credit card." That sounded like a great idea to me!

After we ordered one hooker to fuck us both, he also suggested I try the blow. He said something about lasting longer in the sack and not getting ripped off or being a minute man. I didn't know a whole lot about sex. At that time, I had been with three or four girls only.

In my misery, I said, "Fuck it. I'll do it." And I did my first line. Honestly, I didn't feel much. I didn't understand what all the rage was about. To me it sucked, kind of like weak-ass crank. Regardless of the feeling (probably numb), I kept doing it.

Shortly after, there was a knock on my door. After the paranoia wore off, I answered it and let the hooker in. Brant had been nice enough to let me hit it first. So, she came in and I immediately took her into my bedroom.

She got naked. I bent over the mirror for one more line. After I sniffed it up my nose and the numbness flowed down the back of my throat, I started to undo my belt.

Before I could unbuckle it, I went into a seizure. Flopping around like a fucking fish out of water— foaming out the mouth and all.

She ran out of the room, grabbed the phone off the counter and called 911. Then she dashed outside to her pimp and told him what had happened. She was gone before the cops came. Her clothes still on my floor.

Meanwhile, I was dead.

Yep, according to the medical examiner I was flat-lined and they brought me back.

I don't know for how long or any of that. I just know I was dead. I didn't see light or dark. It was just over and I don't remember anything. Maybe it was because of the drugs or maybe that's how it ends. I don't have an answer for you.

I woke up some time later handcuffed to the hospital bed. After a few clinks of the chain, a nice cop came in and read me my rights. He said as soon as I was released, I was going to jail.

After the drugs wore off and I was in jail, a detective came to me and asked me to snitch on my source. I told them I would and they let me out without bond.

Soon as I got out, I hit the payphone down the road, beeped C-Pain and told him they let me out to snitch, *who did he have a beef with*? He left my 19-year old, dumb white ass faster than a shark on a seal. We never spoke again.

I was fucked and now on the run due to not cooperating. The cops got my folks to convince me to turn myself in. My mom was getting pretty good at sending me to jail, so I fell for it. Again.

Sitting in the county jail with a $25,000 bond at 19 years old. It was almost two months before my grandma finally came to my rescue and got me out. You never know freedom until you don't have it.

Chapter 7: The Longest Day Ever, Part 1

After I got out, I wanted to straighten up. I really did. I moved home with my folks again for about two weeks, worked two jobs and saved enough money to get my own apartment.

I still didn't have a car, though. So, I became the customer service guy at a Mexican restaurant across the street from my apartment. It paid $6.25 an hour and I worked 5-10pm for six days a week. That was just one of my jobs.

My main job paid $9 an hour and it was across town. It was getting harder and harder to find rides to work at 7:30am. There was no public transit and the office was at least four miles from my apartment. It was beginning to look like I had to drop the better paying job or get fired.

I went into the office to talk to the head boss. After I explained my situation, he told me I could work on an apartment job and the apartment boss would pick me up each morning.

I was glad to have a solution. I had to quit my other job, and I wouldn't be home until 6pm each day, but at least I had been able to keep the higher paying one.

The apartment boss wasn't too happy about picking me up.

Even though he lived less than a quarter mile from me, he must have really enjoyed his alone time. OR…he didn't like me.

One of the things this company did to save money was hire guys out of the halfway house. They would all ride in together in a van and then be picked up at the end of the day.

I worked on the job for several months. The boss hated me and pushed me way hard those summer months. I hated it, but I swore to stay clean. It was killing me.

Most of the felons who worked on the job, quit right after they left the halfway house. Some due to location, some due to transportation and some for the fuck of it.

It was actually rare for any of them to be around for any period of time after they left the halfway house. I was constantly training new guys on how to do shit.

One guy, Roy, stuck around. I watched him get a car, new wheels, new clothes, new jewelry and the works. I worked pretty close with him and we got along well.

One day, I asked him, "Man, I know I make more than you, how do you afford all this nice shit?" He said, "I hustle, man. I keep this job as a cover."

I went on to ask him what kind of drugs and prices. He offered to front me and put me in business. "Only one thing," he said. "I'll kill you and your family if you rip me off."

*****

After a few months of working with Roy, I got in good with him. He trusted me with more and more shit. Had me do cool stuff with him and we got along well.

He often paid for me to get in the strip club and for all my dances and drinks at only 20 years old. He had my back; I had his.

One day, about 4pm, I met him at a strip club in Dallas. After a few drinks and dances, we walked out to his car and did our business.

I took several pounds of weed, an amount of coke and crank all in one scoop. No briefcase. No fancy bag, just all this shit laying out in the wide open trunk of Brant's car.

My buddy, Tracey was with me, too. I had been drinking and I wanted to smoke some weed. So, I pinched one of the pounds and got enough weed to roll up a blunt.

After I rolled it, I handed the leftovers to Tracey to keep. I put them in a cigarette cellophane and he stuffed it in his pocket. He didn't really smoke, but he didn't mind keeping it either.

Before we went to the strip club, Brant got us some 40s from the store. He had a fake ID he'd had made in Detroit at some point. It came in handy.

The dirty ride was about 25 miles. It was only two cities over. I was a fucking idiot. I'd never used bags or any of that shit. I'd always just thrown the shit in the trunk and made the driver drive cool, but not that night.

Due to the bitches in the strip club taking my 20-year old attention, I was not thinking. This time, I was distracted. I was riding in a car in which the driver had a fake ID; there was good quantity of three different types of drugs; we had open alcohol containers and I was out on felony bail bond and not even twenty-one. Yet, I decided it was a good time to spark that blunt up.

About the time the blunt was turning into a roach, I had to piss. It came on so quickly I almost pissed myself. At 20, I wasn't used to drinking 40 oz. of beer in 10 minutes. My bladder was about to explode.

I told Brant, "Dude, pull the fuck over. I gotta piss like a racehorse!" He said, "Man, you know we gotta go straight home. We can't get off the freeway." I told him, "I don't give a fuck. I'm pulling my dick out and pissing in your car, or you're pulling into a 7-Eleven."

Reluctantly, he exited the highway into an unfamiliar neighborhood and it took us a few miles off the road to find a store. Finally, as he pulled into the store, I went to put the blunt out. When he parked, I opened the door and smoke poured out.

And of all the cars, which could pull in to grab a few items from the store, the one that did, happened to have "POLICE" written across the side of it. "Motherfucker!" I said, as it was too late to do anything. Not to mention, I still had to piss!

The cop politely smiled and told me to step back into the car. He asked if we had any more drugs on us besides the roach. I told Tracey to give him what he had in his pocket. He was fucking furious! The cops cuffed and arrested him.

I thought it better to get Tracey arrested for a few grams of weed than for all of us to face life for the bulk that was in the trunk. The cops ran all our IDs and put Tracey in the back of the cop car.

They searched the car and there was nothing else inside. Just as they were about to pull away with Tracey in tow, one cop said, "I almost forgot, pop the trunk."

I had a flashback to New Mexico. I knew I was caught.

What should I do?

Gangster shit and run for it?

Take my charge?

What?

As I sat there in a drunken, stoned, full-of-piss state, I heard, "Officer down!! Officer down!!" come across the radio. The address must have been close because they cut Tracey loose and shut the trunk without even opening it.

All the cop said was, "You're fucking lucky. If I see you again, your ass is going to jail. Get out of this neighborhood."

My only problem at that point was that I still had to piss! FML.

Brant backed up, pulled out of the parking lot and headed towards the freeway. He was screaming and Tracey was punching me from the backseat.

I talked Brant into pulling over a few streets down and I pissed in someone's side yard. As we got back on the street, we passed those two cops.

They looked back at us, but didn't turn around. Our hearts were racing. We hit the freeway and finally made it to one of my drop houses.

As soon as we got there my beeper went off.

Chapter 8: The Longest Day Ever, Part 2

Back in the day, we had beeper codes. This was before caller ID. Each of us had a unique code like 6969, which identified who it was. Mine was 404. My girlfriend's was 107.

When my beeper went off with 107-911, I knew something was up.

I called the number and some dude answered, "Sup?" he asked.

I thought, *what a punk! Who the fuck answers the phone like that?*

"Yo, my girl beeped me, is she still there?"

"Who's your girl?"

"The brunette." (Her two best friends were blondes and I didn't know if this dude needed to know her name. After all, she beeped me 911).

"Hold on, fool."

When she got on the phone she said softly, "These dudes are being dicks and won't give me my car keys to leave." I about flipped my lid. My heart still racing from the cop incident only a few minutes before. "What do you mean they won't give you your keys? Where you at?"

She wasn't sure the exact address, but she gave me cross streets. I rounded up three of my homies who were at the drop house, left the drugs there and headed out to find her.

My boys looked skinny like me, but we weren't nothin' to fuck with. We'd seen our fair share of shit go down and been involved in more than we should have. Fighting was kind of our thing. Especially being involved in the drug trade.

We took two cars just in case shit went down and searched the area. Once we found my girl's car, we turned the lights off and parked two doors away. I told them I would go to the door and for them to hang off to the side, out of sight. If at all possible, I didn't want any trouble. We'd had enough for one night.

I knocked on the door and a kid about 15 years old answered. He was the same dude I'd talked to on the phone. I recognized his voice. I asked if he'd go get my girl and out of nowhere, some dude flew past the guy at the door and threw a punch at me.

"WHAT THE FUCK?!?" I yelled, as I realized the dude swung, but had missed me due to his momentum. He sped past me down the porch steps and turned around, planning to jump me from behind as the guy at the door distracted me. But me and my boys got him!

Two of my boys grabbed him and were beating the shit out of him. He was squealing and probably regretting his whole "OUTTA NOWHERE" routine.

Meanwhile, the dude at the door was in shock. He was just a little guy, so I didn't want to hit him, but if he took one step I was gonna drop him.

I managed to spot my girl and her two friends off in the back of the house. These guys' dad must have been home because he came to the door after hearing his son scream.

Then the dad immediately pulled the same act as his son!

He took a swing at me and missed and then his forward motion took him down the stairs, where he suffered the same fate as his son. So far, the score was us-2, them-0. The little guy at the door hollered and I'll be damned if two more brothers didn't come out swinging.

After the first two, I felt like I could read this family's battle plan pretty easily. Run, swing, miss. Fairly simple. As I saw one of the two other brothers, or friends, or whatever coming towards the door, fists cocked, I stepped to the side and pushed the first one down the stairs.

By now, three of my homies had beat the shit out of two of them and were working on the third, while I still hadn't even thrown a punch. Teamwork baby! As the last "big" brother ran out, I decked him right in the fucking temple. Before he could think or blink, his lights went out.

The girls ran to their car, and after I gave my chick an exotic movie scene kiss, drove off so they didn't miss curfew, which was why they had been panicked in the first place.

At some point in the fight, behind my back, some serious shit had gone down that I wasn't privy to yet. John, one of my long-time homies, had pulled a knife and tried to stab one of the guys. When he had, the other guy tripped him and he fell right on his own knife…in his ass!

Seriously, I almost shit myself laughing at the guy. "John, what the fuck did you need a knife for, you sadistic fuck?" "Man I was just being careful in case shit got out of control. Fucking idiot."

We rolled up in John's brand new truck with his ass blood all over the seat. Of course they were cloth seats. He'd been stabbed, pissed off and best of all, he'd started lying his ass off.

He swore they had a knife and stabbed him, which is why he pulled his: "They stabbed me in the ass man, those fucking Mexicans." Keep in mind, John is Persian. Lol.

We drove John to his house, and we didn't realize it, but his mom was home. She saw us come through the door, covered in blood, and flipped the fuck out.

"My baby! My baby! Goddammit Ryan, I knew you were gonna get him killed. I swear to God..."

She was freaked the fuck out. Mad as hell at me. No one wants to blame their kid, so it was always my fault. I got used to taking the blame; it was no sweat off my back anymore. I said, "I'm sorry, but what do you want me to do?"

"Call 911, get him to the ER!!!"

She didn't know it, but she lived in a house full of drugs. There was no way I was going to call 911, nor was she. I said, "Fine, I'll take him to the ER. Come on John, dumbass."

Brant drove and I sat with John in the back seat, while asking him repeatedly if he wanted me to rub his ass. He kept calling me a fag and ducking his head in shame. He knew we knew...

When we arrived at the hospital, we went right in and told the biggest lie we could concoct. The problem is, we hadn't really coordinated our stories much. All of the excitement caused us to miss this one important detail.

Immediately upon seeing the stab wound, the ER nurse called the police and got them there to take an official report. John was too hard headed to tell them it was an accident that he'd had on his own. Instead, he told the cops he'd gotten jumped at a gas station in the east part of town.

The cop wasn't buying it at all. None of our stories added up.

Finally, when the cop got to me, I shot him straight. After I told him my story he said, "Good thing you said something, because I was about to arrest all of you guys. Look in that room over there. See those guys? They said you came to their house and beat the shit out of them tonight. After their story and your story, I'm gonna call it even and call it a night. Good luck. Tell your buddies you saved their asses."

When they finally discharged John from the ER with 16 stitches in his ass, we headed home. We ran into the cop in the parking lot. He had been waiting for us, and he warned us not to fuck around in his town again. Then he made sure he had all our info in his notebook for future reference.

It looked like we were in the clear. Except I still had a house full of drugs I needed to get to the final drop spot and it was getting later and later. Everyone knew not to move dope at night. Everyone but me.

Chapter 9: The Longest Day Ever, Part 3

Once we got to John's house we greeted his mom and assured her he was all good. We needed her to calm down in order to sneak the big ass bags of weed and other shit out.

After about an hour or so, his mom finally took her ass to bed and passed out. We snuck all the drugs out and headed to the final spot in Dallas.

This spot was sketchy as fuck. I used it as my drop and trap house because it was in a part of town that cops didn't even patrol. Yes, even the cops were scared of getting shot there. It was the perfect place to hold dope. As long as you had guns, these fools would jack you in a heartbeat.

To give you an idea of how bad this 'hood was, let me describe to you, a scene that I witnessed firsthand in the summer of 2000.

It was late as fuck or early as fuck, depending on how you see it. Regardless, let's call it 4 am. I'm all tweaked out on meth one night, still up chillin' with a couple of strippers in the apartment.

I'm sitting by the window getting a blow job and the lights from a helicopter shine right through the sliding glass window, piercing through those old school blinds that just hang there and only move when the wind blows.

I jumped up so quick that the chick who was blowing me scraped the fuck out of my cock. I went midnight to six o'clock in .0003 seconds. I thought the cops were raiding me.

I was small potatoes in this 'hood and there was no way the cops could have been on to me, but drugs and cops equal paranoia. Like any dumb-ass tweaker, I peered out the blinds and saw some shit lookin' like it came straight out of a movie.

A black dude was running through the parking lot right outside my sliding glass door. He jumped up on top of the brick wall that signified the property boundary and right on top of the wall, the dude opened fire on the cops chasing him!

Then the crazy fuck did a back flip off the wall and I don't think he was even shot once. I shit you not, I lost my fucking mind. Seeing this shit was way better than a blow job. I was glad we'd gotten interrupted. This was just one glimpse of how life was in this 'hood.

So, after the drugs, cops, an ass stabbing and momma drama, we had made it to the spot. I've always been a backup plan man. That being said, about one block away I had another spot to get to quick in the event of an emergency.

If there is anything I learned from that night the helicopter scared the shit out of me, it was to never sleep or party where the dope is. Least not any quantity of it anyway.

Also after that fateful helicopter-ish night, I decided never to be anywhere without guns. That dude could have come in my place and shot me up. If I shot him first, I could have been a hero. Hero = no search and seizure.

When I unlocked the door of the next place, I saw a packed house. The front opened right into the living room of this 500 square foot apartment. Every single inch of this place was occupied. Every seat had an ass. Two people were up, pacing.

In a time before easy access cell phones and texts, all people had to rely on was, "Where the fuck you been?" and all they knew was what you told them.

I didn't have time to explain it all, didn't think they would believe me and I surely didn't need all these paranoid weirdos on my shit if I narked. So, I just got down to business.

"I'm late. Fuck it. What do you guys need?"

A few of the dudes (there were probably eight total and two chicks) walked into the kitchen behind me and started putting in their orders. I had to cut, weigh and bag the shit, so it was going to take a minute.

While I was doing my thing, some chick named Kristy came into the kitchen. She was a young stripper who three or four of my homeboys were trying to fuck, but far as I knew none had hit it yet. My girlfriend didn't need to know she was there and it didn't matter.

She was being super flirty with me and we smoked a blunt while I did my thing. She kept touching me and I knew the signals. I felt like a badass. Drugs. Guns. Bitches.

Winning…but not really.

After I got done weighing all the orders up and collecting cash, I went into the living room and sat down. Most of the ten people that had been there were gone. It was starting to mellow out.

It was me, the stripper chick, Randy, Brant and Gary. Gary lived there and I worked with Randy. Gary had just bought a brand new .367 Magnum with one of those five-inch barrels that looks tough as fuck.

This gun was chrome with black handles and would hold five or six bullets in the chamber. Most of all, it was intimidating as fuck when it was pulled on someone.

I picked up the gun, checked to see if it was unloaded and then fired a dry round with the barrel pointed at the door. I was high as fuck at this point on weed, Xanax, alcohol and adrenaline. Not to mention trying to be cool, so I could bang this chick in a short while.

I repeated the process a few times and probably rattled off some bullshit tough guy sayings as I fired each dry round. After a bit, I sat the gun down, got up and went to take a piss in the bathroom.

It was 1am or later on a Saturday morning, the apartment was filled with dudes so high and tweaked out, they were afraid to drive home. I figured my work for the day was done.

After I came out of the bathroom and took my place back on the couch, I picked up the gun. It was in the same spot I'd left it and I assumed no one had touched it.

I pulled the hammer and before anyone could say anything, fired a live round right through the front door. That's right. Gunshots, drugs and tweakers. I might as well have stirred up a human anthill.

Turns out, this dude named Chad was coming to get more weed and right as the shot was fired he knocked on the door. He swore he saw the bullet fly by his head and lodge into the pillar supporting the neighbor's balcony.

To put it lightly, he was mad as fuck. Thought we were trying to kill him over the $500 he was bringing us that he owed. I'm lucky this shit didn't turn into a 1am gun battle of tweakers in the 'hood.

While I had been in the bathroom, that asshole Randy had reloaded the gun and hadn't told anyone. FUCK!!!

After I calmed Chad down in 4.5 seconds, I scrambled to the kitchen to gather all the dope up and put it in trash bags. Scales, pipes, papers and all other evidence had to go.

Live gun shots meant cops were coming soon!

As I ran outside and piled the two or three bags of shit into the work truck we had, the neighbor from the balcony above started screaming something I can only assume was Arabic.

The corner of this complex where our unit was had four doors all facing the same direction. Stacked on top of each other, two floors each. You couldn't fart without the other three neighbors knowing it happened. Due to the high crime rates in the area, everyone was always on high alert.

I looked up to the neighbor and yelled, "Hey man, chill the fuck out. My drunk-ass friends blew a firework off in the house." He said, "Oh yeah, well what the fuck is that hole in your door and chunk missing from that pillar, and what's in that bag?"

"You got a lot of questions for a stranger, dude. Never mind my business. I suggest you go back inside." Which he did immediately. I hopped in the truck and drove one block over and unloaded the haul in the back up house.

Fat Mike lived in the back up house. He flipped out when I busted in without warning and dropped my shit off in a safe that I kept there. I gave him some free crank to get him to chill for a moment.

Then I left the drop house and went back by the spot and fixed the hole in our door with black electrical tape. It fit perfectly since the door was painted black. Then I dug the slug out of the pillar at the neighbor's.

Lastly, I grabbed the stripper and asked if she and I could chill at her house. She said, "Grab meth and weed. Let's go."

When we got back to her house, she started undressing, slipped into the bathtub and started doing all sorts of fun stuff to herself. About the time I was going to jump in and join her, there was a knock on her door.

"Jesus fucking Christ, it's 2:30am, who the fuck is here? Do you think it's the cops?" She told me to calm down, but I wasn't hearing it.

I grabbed my gun out of my bag and looked through the peephole. It was one of the guys who bought dope from me named Primo and he said, "Let me in, man."

I opened the door and was like, "What the fuck you doing here? Did you follow me?"

He replied, "Naw man, I live across the hall, been up on some of your new shit and saw you come in with the neighbor girl. FYI buddy, you ain't the only one she brings over here, if you know what I'm saying."

"Of fucking course I know, you dipshit. She's a goddamned stripper, not a Catholic nun."

He replied, "Oh, well that makes sense."

Finally, after about 20 minutes, I convinced him to go away and gave him some free dope. Not five minutes later, we heard another knock on the door!

This time, it was one of the dudes from the trap house we'd been at earlier, and he was trying to creep. When he saw me, we talked for a few and then he split.

Meanwhile that bathwater must have gotten cold, because the chick was not there when I showed back up. She was in bed, naked and gave me the "come hither" finger gesture. It was on.

After the worst day ever, I needed some pussy and she had just the right amount for me. Besides, every good story needs a happy ending.

Chapter 10: Prison Purgatory, Part 1

The time between January 19, 1999 and November 11, 2000 was a wild time in my life. Much like purgatory, I was waiting to either go on to probation or to prison, but I wasn't sure which would be in my future.

Due to this internal confusion and struggle, I did just about every dumb-ass thing you can think of as my own personal way of self-sabotaging my life. Much like the longest day ever, I did a lot of stupid shit that could have left me locked up to this day.

Allow me to set the tone, scene and mood for you.

My grandma had spent her own money to bail me out of jail on a $25,000 bond. I was running the streets selling dope to pay my bills. I weighed probably 130 pounds soaking wet and I'm only 5' 10" tall. You can believe that everywhere I went, I took my gun with me. Or two...

Since I've been about 12 years old, I've remembered my family always saying, "Ryan, keep that shit up and one day you'll be going to prison." I kind of felt like it was my duty to prove them right.

After being abandoned, adopted, on drugs, beaten and all that other fun stuff, I hadn't realized how much pain I had tucked away in the back of my mind. I've never lived in the past. Yet I've always tried to find ways to destroy my future.

I was confident I was going to end up in prison. From the moment I'd gotten caught, I always just felt the penitentiary was in my future. With this lingering in my mind at all times, I would do anything to escape it. Fights, drugs, sex and any other degenerate shit you can think of, I'd do. Just as a way to self-inflict pain and self-destruct.

One day, Brant hit me up.

He said his parents were going out of town and they'd given him the keys to their house to keep an eye on it. To both of us, that meant party time!

Funny thing about Brant's parents, Brant and his brother were both fuck ups and Brant had them convinced he was the more trustworthy of the two. Truth is, he was the worst. Almost every time we were left the house, he called his older brother to come party with us.

His brother was only two years older, and lived about 20 minutes away in another city. He always had cool drugs and some interesting people around. We liked to party with him.

I was at Brant's house when his parents told us, "Guys, you can do whatever you want. We know you're going to party, just don't drink our wine. It's expensive and some of it is irreplaceable. If you drink even one bottle we will fucking kill you. Understood?" Brant's stepdad was 6' 6" and 240 pounds, he got his point across easily.

So, here we were, left alone in the house, only rule was don't touch the wine. Easy enough.

First thing we did was call for a ride. At the time, neither of us owned a car. Brant still semi-lived at home. After my overdose, we'd gotten kicked out of our apartment and he'd moved back home to save cash, but rarely slept there.

I had an apartment about three miles up the road from his parent's house. It had two couches and a TV. One couch in the living room to watch TV on, and another in the bedroom to sleep on. I was living in fucking poverty.

Most days, I didn't have food in my cupboard. I had a little cash, but no ability to understand credit or how to buy a car. The nearest grocery store was five miles away. That meant if I went and bought food it was 10 miles round trip.

I was not smart enough to know I had good credit and could buy a car. Hell, I didn't even know that I could call a taxi. I just didn't know. No one had taught me and I didn't think of it on my own. So, I mostly just ordered delivery food. Which in reality, gets expensive AND boring very quickly.

I say all of this, because the fucking prospect of staying at Brant's parent's house with food, a bed and a party, sounded like fucking heaven about right then.

I had hooked up with this chick, Patricia. Her mom was a teacher and had heard about me. She hated me. Patricia loved me, though. She liked my bad boy style and sometimes, she would let me use her car.

I called her up and asked if she would take a few of us to get some beer. She didn't drink, but she was down to help us out. None of us were 21, so it was a risk on her end to drive with alcohol.

She showed up to Brant's house in her Chevy S-10 Blazer and scooped us up. Brant had a fake ID, so we headed to the store.

I don't know if I've mentioned it yet, but Brant looks like Pee Wee Herman on meth. He has real dark hair on his head, eyebrows and arms, but is pale as shit. He was skinny as fuck, too. Probably weighed 120 and was 5' 8". He always wore his

JNCO jeans about five sizes too big. So, no way did he look twenty-one. More like twelve.

It took us a few stores before we could finally buy some beer. We had about $40 on us, so we got two cases of Keystone. About 48 beers for three of us dudes. That's never how it works, though.

We got back to Brant's folks' house and spied the neighbors leaving out the back door and down the alley. They had come from Brant's backyard. Brant's folks and the neighbors were good friends, so Brant said, "They were probably just checking things out."

Patricia dropped us off and said she had to work or some shit. She would be back around midnight when she got off.

Then it was just three dudes and 48 beers.

When you are 19 or so, beer gets you drunk faster and with less of a hangover. Your young body can process shit quickly. We were about three beers in when we started feeling the buzz.

"Hey man, let's call some chicks over."

"I'll call my older brother and see what he's got going on," Brant responded.

"Call Christian and see what girls he's with. Tell him we got beer."

Christian was this bad ass dude who never did drugs, but could drink like a fish. He could fight, had sleeve tattoos at 18 and was pretty fucking good at motocross. Because of his handsomeness, rumored 11-inch cock and racing career, he always had some fine girlfriend who had hot friends.

Brant, being the dumb-ass he is, called not only Christian, but he went ahead and called his older brother, too. I like Brant's brother, but he didn't have any chicks and he never rolled alone. That meant more assholes who would want to share our beer.

Since Brant had been nice enough to invite every dude we knew over, we still needed chicks. I had a girl, but at the same time, I was not married, lol. I also didn't like and still don't like the atmosphere of all dudes. I need females around or it's just weird.

About 8pm it started getting dark, and people began arriving. I have no idea how long or how many beers we had drank, but we were feeling it. Christian showed up with a girl. Brant's bro brought three dudes and said they had other friends coming, too. No chicks.

I pulled Brant off to the side and said, "Man what kind of shit party is this? Who are you gonna blow here? I mean you gotta be wanting to blow someone, you invited all these dudes." He was steaming mad in a way that only I could incite.

About 9:30pm, I was in the other room when I heard a scuffle in the living room. I was stoned and pretty drunk at this point. Maybe even on Xanax, too. Regardless, some shit went down in the living room.

This is exactly why I hate drinking with just dudes. Because one of them had gotten drunk enough to rile the others up and get them to do dumb shit things. Brant's bro's pals didn't know that Christian was a bad mother fucker. They only saw some skinny dude with tattoos.

One of the guys hit on Christian's girl while he went to piss. When he came back and saw it, he immediately, without question, hit the dude and dropped him. Brant's bro was yelling at him and about to be next in line to get dropped.

About that time, I looked over and saw the wine missing from where Brant's parents had left it. I asked, "Who drank the wine?" Everyone looked at me like they were stupid.

Christian had hit one dude, now Brant hit the next one!

"Where's my fucking wine, bitch?" BOOM! For a little dude, Brant packed a punch. It was fucking on. The goddamned royal rumble went down right then.

Dudes were pushed out the door and beaten in the yard, too. I don't exactly remember how many people there were, but we were all fighting. Even Christian's girl was pounding on some dude.

After taking a beating for a few minutes that seemed more like a few hours, the dudes made it out of the house, ran to their car and said they would be back. We had started shit we couldn't stop.

Brant was about to go to war with his own damn brother.

Stupid ass drunk dudes.

Before I could even get a grasp on what had happened, we all jumped in Christian's truck and took off after them. Driving 90 mph on the back roads to Wide Awake Wylie, Texas was an insane ride in the bed of a truck being driven by a semi-pro racer.

When Christian caught up to them, he forced them off the road. They got out of the car and we commenced beating on them again. At some point, they got back in the car and drove off. We did a U-turn and headed back for more beer to celebrate our victory.

On the way home, we decided we needed more beer, but had no money. We were all in agreement that a "beer 'n' go" was our only hope of a continued buzz.

We pulled up to a gas station and Brant ran in. He grabbed two cases, one in each hand. Then he walked up to the counter, looked the guy right in the eye and said, "This is me stealing your beer, bitch! WOO HOO!!!!" When he ran out, we drove off.

Normally, that would be where it ended. Not this guy. He must have been the owner of the store or some shit because he was furious. He followed Brant out the door and hopped in a tow truck with lights on top.

He left the entire store wide open to chase us over two cases of beer!

I looked back and saw that he even had the yellow lights flashing. He was in hot pursuit and had probably called the cops on his car phone. FUCK.

Christian knew how to drive, though. He was getting away and quick. He made a sharp right from the left lane and the guy tried to duplicate his move in the tow truck, but dude missed the turn and hit the turn signal in the median, then drove right up the pole. Two wheels off the ground and all. Bent the shit out of the light pole.

About the time he hit the pole, I saw police lights flash. The cops pulled him over. As we drove off I could see him yelling at the cops who had their weapons out...lol. What an idiot.

By the time we made it home to Brant's parent's place it was about 11:30pm. The phone rang and it was Brant's brother talking some shit about coming back over and shooting us.

Fuck! What the fuck had we created? They said they had cuts, bruises and the like. They also told us they knew nothing about the wine. Brant called them fucking liars and hung up.

As promised, around midnight Patricia showed up. She never let me hit it, but she gave me head and we would make out. She was a virgin and I was probably not her first choice to lose it, but she was fun, nonetheless. I heard she turned out to be a softcore porn star. You never know who someone will grow up to be.

We made out, then passed out. About 1:30am, I heard yelling and screaming loud enough to wake me from a dead drunken state. I looked out the window to see three cars out front full of dudes. They were trying to figure out how to get in the house.

I had been asleep in the master bedroom. I knew Brant's big-ass stepdad kept a few rifles in his closet. I got up, ran over to the closet and grabbed two.

I grew up shooting and aside from the longest day incident, had never had an accident. I knew that only one of the guns was loaded. So, I went out the front door and fired a shot in the air. When I threw the unloaded gun to Brant, he had a look on his face of disbelief.

I said, "PUT YOUR FUCKING HANDS ON THE HOOD OF YOUR CAR. WHAT THE FUCK ARE YOU IDIOTS DOING?" I then took the butt of the rifle and struck one of the dudes in the forehead, knocking him down.

Meanwhile, Rick started beating the shit out of another dude. None of the dudes had moved after the warning shot.

Once Rick was done, the dude I hit got up and I calmed the situation down. Everyone agreed to a truce and the guys drove off, back to Wylie, with their tails between their legs.

Meanwhile, all I wanted to do was sleep. Patricia called me a psychopath and yelled at me for an hour before dumping me and finally letting me get back to sleep, in a real bed for once.

I woke up the next morning and realized what all had happened. Dude, the cops hadn't even show up. What in the hell? It had been like 2am when our yelling and gunshots echoed in the middle of a dense neighborhood.

WOW. I was one lucky fuck…again.

I had lost my girl, though. She was hot and I wanted to be her first, but now all of that was over. I was back to being stag.

When I woke up, it must have been around noon. I walked into the living room and noticed Brant had already cleaned everything up. It looked just like when we'd arrived.

It was only the two of us, so I went into the back yard and lit up a joint to reflect on my life and the poor decisions I had made. After a couple of hits, I put it out, then stuffed the rest in my cigarette pack.

When I walked back in, the neighbors were in the living room. I guess this was the day Brant's parents were supposed to come back to town.

Apparently, the neighbors had grabbed the wine and were there returning it. Yes, that means we got in fights, fired shots and hurt people over nothing. The neighbors had grabbed the wine when they were there earlier. We just hadn't noticed at the time.

We never told Brant's brother what happened with the neighbors, but we were never really cool again. FML...

Chapter 11: Prison Purgatory, Part 2

It was around the first weekend of September. In Texas, September is a month of celebration. Dove season opens. It's a long-time Texas tradition to go shoot some birds midflight during the fall.

On opening weekend, everywhere you look it's like an episode of *Duck Dynasty*. Dudes in 4x4s sporting camouflage all over the place. From city slickers to rednecks, they all go hunting for doves when September rolls around.

I don't know about everybody else's family, but where I grew up, you have a few beers, eat some beef jerky and shoot some birds. It's an experience that's meant to be fun.

Just like every other opening weekend, I was pumped and ready to go shoot some birds. I forgot to mention how fucking delicious doves are with bacon wrapped around the breast and a jalapeno in the middle. The shit is money!

This would be the first year I was old enough to go and that I had owned my guns. I met with Brant, John and Rick who had ridden in two separate vehicles to meet at my apartment in Dallas.

In Rick's car, we loaded up two shotguns, an ice chest of beer, a pistol to shoot for fun and in case of snakes and a quarter ounce of weed. It was going to be a bad ass trip and we had it all planned out.

Hunt from 5am to 10am, party all day at the cabin we'd rented, then we would hunt from 5pm to sundown. The place we were headed to had a pond, as well. So, we could fish during the day if we didn't get too hammered.

When Rick showed up at the apartment super early that morning, he showed off his new stereo, some new 12s and a fancy amp. I've never understood how all that shit works, but I liked the way it sounded.

Apparently, Rick had been awake all night hooking up his system. He said he hadn't planned on it being that way, but something hadn't worked right when he'd turned it on, so it had taken him all night to set it up properly.

Of the two vehicles that were at my place, John and Rick were the ones who owned them. Both vehicles, after being loaded with our shit, became two-seaters. In a time when gas was 89 cents a gallon, taking two cars for four people was no big deal.

We smoked a joint, put our shit in the trunk, cranked the car and headed down the freeway to lush fields full of doves a little after five in the morning. Since Rick had the new bad ass car stereo, I elected to ride with him. He was also 21, so he could ride with the beer and my pistol legally.

I should be clear that Rick is a scary bitch. He's such a pussy when it comes to taking responsibility, it's unreal. He's never had to own up to shit in his life. I don't know why I ever hung with that coward.

We got less than five miles down the road when a cop pulled behind us with flashing lights. *What in the actual fuck, man? We weren't speeding. I don't need this shit, man*, I said to myself.

Rick said, "I can't go to jail man, you gotta claim the weed."

We argued for a couple minutes until the cop showed up at the window.

He said, "Did you know you had two tail lights out?"

Rick: "No officer, I just put a stereo in this car, I must have shorted them. I didn't know."

Officer: "Where you guys headed? What's in the cooler?"

Rick: "We are headed to Leonard to shoot some dove. We have some beer in the cooler."

Officer: "You guys have guns in this car? Step out of the vehicle. Are either of you even twenty-one?"

Rick: I'm 22, officer. Yes, we have two shotguns in the trunk. We have not drank any beer. All 24 are still on ice in the cooler."

Officer after cuffing and detaining us: "Soon as I opened the door, I found this marijuana. Whose is it? Anything else in the car I need to know about?"

Rick: "The weed is his and there is nothing else."

Officer: "So let me get this straight. You guys have weed, beer and guns and you are going to operate those guns under the influence at some point?"

Rick: "It's not really like that, you hunt. You know how it is."

Officer: "Rick, is there anything else I need to know about in the car?"

Rick: "No."

The officer tore apart the car, which still makes no sense. He already had guns, weed and beer. I don't know what the fuck else he wanted to find.

Our innocent situation and fun day was quickly being spun into a gun-toting, drug-doing story for some bitch-made cop to be a hero.

The cop came back after searching the car. He looked at me and said, "Is this your pistol?" Before I could get a word out, that bitch Rick said, "Yes, that's his, officer."

This mother fucker was 22 years old, and he had every legal right to have that gun. I was 20, and I had no rights. It was a clean new gun. Instead of claiming it and it being no big deal, he blamed me and I was arrested for unlawful possession of firearm: Class B misdemeanor.

Tie that back in with the weed, and I now had two Class B misdemeanors, so I was whisked off to jail in Plano, Texas at 6am. My opening day was fucked.

I expected John or Rick to come bail me out. It never happened. Those piece of shit motherfuckers went on to my land, camped out and hunted. They never gave a second thought about me.

That day, I learned those guys weren't my friends. They were friends with each other and used me for cash and drugs. It was a hard day for me. One I will never forget.

Here I was, out on bail for a felony, and now in jail again for two more misdemeanors. What was I doing with my life? I'll tell you, I was fucking destroying it—atomic bomb style.

Once I got booked, I made a call to my homie, Bonecrusher. He and another dude, Primo, who bought shit from me, came and bailed me out. Soon as I got out, they took me to my place to get money and drugs to pay them back.

I was back on the streets in about 14 hours, but I was fucking pissed. I swore to God the next time I saw Rick I was going to shoot his bitch ass. I've still not seen him to this day. If you're reading this Rick, fuck off.

My biggest problem at the time was that I was scheduled to go to prison in a couple of months and I was out of money. Dammit, I knew I was gonna have to sell some extra dope to make up for the shit. Seemed like I could never catch a break. Now that I look back, I was just trying to die. I hated myself and life so much, but didn't even recognize it.

I had some connections in New Orleans that had really cheap cocaine, but they didn't get good weed there. Since I needed money quick, I worked out a deal to take some weed to New Orleans in exchange for blow.

Sounded legit. All I had to do was make a 20 hour round trip down some of the most policed freeways in the world, in a vehicle filled with the very substance those police were looking for. Fuck, I was fucking retarded!

But of course, I made the trip, and successfully at that. I even did a little meth to keep me extra awake and paranoid. Two of my "friends" went with me, as well. We made the drop, got the product and went to a hotel.

At the hotel, we packaged the goods up like we wanted and got all situated. My two homeboys were fucked up on meth and didn't want to leave the hotel room. I was losing my mind being trapped in a room with them.

I took the vehicle into the French Quarter and went looking for a party. Soon as I pulled onto one of the side streets I spotted a chick lying on the ground.

Now I'm not a genius, but I know that the streets in the Quarter are nasty as fuck. The chick looked hot and it would only be a minute before something bad happened to her.

As I drove closer, I realized it was my ex-girlfriend—the one that had broken my heart and caused the whole overdose episode to go down.

There she was, fucked up on some drug and lying on the ground. I thought to myself, *there's no more of a guarantee of getting laid, than what is lying on the ground before me.*

I pulled the truck up and yelled for her to get in. She had to rub her eyes at first; she couldn't believe it was me. Then she went on to tell me about how fucked up on Ecstasy she was, how it was a bad night and her friends had bailed on her.

I took her back to the hotel room, we did our thing and then I dropped her off at her friend's house, where she was staying. I got her to promise to meet me back in Dallas in two days.

"I go to court soon, but I'd like to spend my last few days with you." I told her.

The next day, early, we hopped in the truck and us three dudes made the drive back to Texas in once piece with no incident. We made the switch. I made the cash and shit fell into place for once.

It was a Sunday night when we got back to Dallas. Monday morning, my beeper went off. My lawyer. He told me to come into his office because he needed to see me before court that week.

I was barely 21 years old in November of 2000. I wasn't sure what would become of my life. I'm not even sure I really cared.

When I got to my lawyer's office, he told me I was flat busted and had three options. This was a Felony 1 case (same category as murder for $200 worth of coke) and I could do 20 years' probation deferred, 10 years' probation and the charge would be on my record, or 2 years in prison.

"Now Ryan, I want you to consider something. You're not even 22 years old yet, and you've been to jail a half dozen times already. Twenty years' probation is a huge risk for you, same with ten years. I recommend you take the two years in jail. It's your first offense; you will stay in the county for four months and make parole. You'll never see a prison yard. Just my advice."

I had five days to sort it out and meet him in court.

In those five days, I tried to fuck my ex as much as possible. I wasn't going to get pussy for a while, so I was trying to catch up.

One night, her car got towed from my parking spot. The whole ordeal ended up costing me $600 that I didn't have.

Goddamned bad luck was bleeding me to death.

I tried to reason with the tow truck driver, but he didn't give a fuck. We ended up getting even with him later. (In a few ways, but that doesn't belong in this book.)

In the short time I had to get my shit together, I packed my stuff and put it in storage. I also made the decision I would never fuck with drugs again.

I introduced John to my connection and John promised to pay me $100 per week by way of money on my books. I also told my connection that I was out. No one would ever hear from me again. I was done for real this time.

They respected me because they knew I didn't snitch ever. I'm sure they figured I would be back, though. Ralf and Juan were good dudes to me.

On November 11, 2000, I woke up, fucked my ex one more time, then got into the shower. I put on a t-shirt, a dress shirt, pants and nice shoes. It was cold as fuck outside, so I wore my heavy camouflage coat. Then one of my homies drove me to the courthouse.

Chapter 12: Let's Go to Prison

One of the reasons I chose to go to prison was because a lot my friends were dying. Reggie was shot 23 times by the Dallas police; Nate died, coked out of his mind on a four wheeler; one of the electrical guys hung himself with wire right in front of me; another shot up, overdosed and died while I was on the job, and of course, I already told you about Shad who'd overdosed on heroin.

I needed to dry out of drugs, get my mind right and focus on what I was going to do when I was released. Plus, I figured four months in county jail would be a breeze and I'd get it together by then.

I went to court that morning and all my family was there. I hadn't spoken to, or invited any of them, but they came anyway. My grandparents, stepdad, mom, sister, my other grandma, all of them were present, except for my real dad, who was on the road somewhere.

My lawyer told me, "Good morning, now take that stupid camouflage jacket off and put this Visine in your eyes. I can't believe you would show up to court high."

"Dude, chill. I got a lot of heavy shit going on today, man.

It's my last time." I told him.

I took my jacket off and walked into the courtroom ahead of my family, alongside my lawyer. I looked the judge in the eye and admitted my guilt. He told me I was to be sentenced to two years in a state penitentiary for felony manufacturing delivery of a controlled substance over 3 grams but less than 250 grams. A Felony 1 carries 5-99 years, but he would make an exception for me due to my first time and age.

As soon as the gavel slammed, the bailiff came over and cuffed me. I was able to look back and see my entire family in tears. I had no time for that; I couldn't worry about them anymore.

I had to worry about me.

*****

After the cuffs were slapped on me, I was whisked away to a door in the side of the courtroom. You know. The one they always use on courtroom TV shows when they bring out the dude in cuffs and orange. That one.

Inside that door, they stripped me naked in front of two cops. They took my belt, wallet, jewelry, earrings, shoes, clothes and even my boxers. I was given a green jumpsuit with snaps in the front. I had to go commando inside this suit.

To make matters worse, I was handcuffed again and sat in a cage for what seemed like days, but I assume were really hours. I had no watch, no clock to see and didn't want to ask the guards because it didn't matter.

When the time came, I was escorted harshly onto the bus by the jailers. The bus took me back to the same county jail I had already been to twice. I was sort of familiar with the system at this point, so I knew what to expect, which was a long night of sitting in a plastic chair with nothing to eat, in a jumper with my dick hanging out one of the snaps. Fuck!

Not to mention it was November and cold as fuck inside the county jail. This is no ordinary county jail, though. It was originally built to be high security, a one-of-a-kind federal holding facility, (which it is now), but the crooked ass sheriff who owned the land ended up using it for the county once he got re-elected.

What I'm saying is this county jail was fucking state of the art. Even by today's standards. It was spotless clean, quiet and heavily guarded.

There were two tiers of cells. Each cell on the bottom held two men; each cell on top held one man. About 60 cells made up each tier. The cells faced the dayroom and a guard who stood behind a pulpit like Captain Kirk, all the while opening and closing doors for inmates.

This jail had three clusters that each had four pods. It was big as shit and the hallways were long. Outside each pod, in the middle of the cluster, was an operating room that had guards in it, but you couldn't see them due to the window tint. They watched videos of inmates all day and night in there and controlled what was called the sally ports.

After a few days of adjusting, getting poked by needles, blood drawn, immunizations, examinations and all that bull shit, I got settled in. I kept to myself except when I would meet someone who was back from prison. Then I'd ask them questions just in case I had to go.

Likewise, county jail sucked. I watched all these guys come and go. Get arrested, stay a day and make bond. It's hard to do time while you're witnessing people leave constantly. The last thing you want to think about is the outside or going home, especially in the beginning.

About two months into my stay at the county hotel, I got a call on the speaker in my cell at three in the morning.

"Inmate Stewman."

"Yes?"

"Get dressed, get your shit and get packed. You're on the chain."

"What the fuck does the chain mean?"

Silence.

I turned around and my celly had a smirk on his face. "Bro, you're headed to prison. Good luck with that."

I did what the guard told me and then pushed the button to exit my cell. Sleepy as fuck and unprepared, I was headed to God knows where in the dark night. Needless to say, I was fucking frightened.

I was about to find out, firsthand, if all those stories about prison were true.

I carried my shit down this long-ass hallway back to booking. As soon as I got there, I noticed the

Texas Department of Corrections guards standing nearby.

These guys were huge, had cowboy hats on and did not look like they were there to fuck around. "Where the fuck you been, Stewman?" one of them yelled at me. I noticed a gang of other inmates had beaten me to book-in.

I went to tell them that I had only five-minutes notice and it was the CO's fault, but they interrupted me and were not trying to hear excuses. The hazing process had begun and it was intimidating as fuck.

They stripped me butt naked, threw my shit in a bag and told me all I needed to bring was my balls. I was gonna need a big set being a white boy. I threw a white sleeveless jumper on that was dirty as fuck, smelled like piss and again, went commando.

They then chained me (hence the name, "the chain") to the other inmates. I was alongside some dude who was twice my size looking like he was straight out of the Aryan brotherhood. Covered in tats and not seeming like I could get on his good side.

They gave us a little speech before they got us on the bus at gunpoint.

"Alright you fucking scumbags. Yeah, that's right, I said scumbags. The fine state of Texas says you guys are lawbreaking scumbags. So much to the point that you have to be locked away from society. Now let's get a few things straight. This is my bus. I've been running this bus for 30 years, every fucking week, you cocksuckers. Oh yeah, within 24 hours, studies show that 20 percent of you motherfuckers will be certified cocksuckers. Hope you like black dick in your mouths..."

Now...what was I saying...? Oh, yeah...this is my bus, 30 years and no escaped convicts. Which is a damned shame because I'm a good shot and I'd love to get to kill one of you cocksuckers and be a news' hero at the same time. Don't make my fucking dreams come true today. You're going to get on that bus. You're going to shut the fuck up and you are going to do exactly what we tell you.

You will be strapped to your partner here, or lover, or whatever you two fags cuffed together are. Regardless, you gotta piss, he's gotta hold your dick. There will be no shitting on my bus. If I have to smell your shit, you will regret it. We clear? Get on the fucking bus, NOW!"

Chapter 13: Welcome to the House of Hate

All the movies in the world couldn't have prepared me for what I was about to experience over the next 20 months. I shit you not. It was nothing like I'd expected, but everything I hoped it wouldn't be.

After we got on that bus, we stopped and picked up inmates from two or three other local county jails. Some of the surrounding counties to Collin County are not as nice and suburban. There were some rough dudes on that bus.

About four hours in and unbeknownst to me at the time, 45 minutes away from the prison, the guards stopped at McDonald's and went in. I sat there thinking they were getting us food for a long trip. I was still so young and dumb.

The main guard who yelled at us in the beginning, began again:

"You cocksuckers see this?" The guard pointed to his Big Mac. "This is the last time you will see any shit like this again for a long time, some of you never again. Fuck each one of you scumbags. I want you to sit here and watch me eat it and enjoy it. Freedom never tasted so good, you cocksuckers."

It was like a scene from the movie *Full Metal Jacket*. When we finally turned in down that 300-yard strip that led to the prison sally port, it hit me.

This shit was real. I was in Tennessee Colony, Texas—home to six state prisons. One had pork, one chicken, one created textiles, two grew vegetables and one had a trucking division.

They all supported each other, of course, by way of inmate slavery.

Speaking of slavery. I'm no racist, and I don't even feel like I have to justify anything I say to you. Just so we are clear, I don't give a fuck about how you feel about how I feel. That being said, I'm not racist. I was thrown in prisons where the racism happened to me, and I was the minority. Don't misconstrue anything or any of the stories I'm about to tell you and direct them toward one race or the other. Prison, and the world in general, is full of idiots. Prison just has a higher concentration.

I saw all these gigantic, archaic looking prisons with weird names, and I was taken to one called Gurney that looked like it was made out of a series of barns lined up alongside each other, metal roofs and all.

We pulled into the sally port and the bus started unloading. After I got off the bus, I saw a dude from behind me we had picked up at another jail, who had no legs and rolled in in a wheelchair, get kicked off the bus and forced to crawl on his elbows into the sally port.

It was fierce to see. Turned out the guy killed a family of four while drunk driving and that's how he lost his legs...so fuck him anyway. The guards knew it and they were going to make his life miserable.

We were all stripped naked and forced to stand nuts to butts together in line waiting for our head to be shaved, our picture to be taken and a shower. They had a goddamned assembly line set up for us. Coming from the car wash business, I had some sort of weird admiration for the organization.

I had already shaved my head so I was good. I got in the shower, cleaned up, then was handed boxers, two pants, two white shirts, two t-shirts, a jacket, two pairs of socks, boots and a mattress.

I was given my pod assignment. After I was dressed, I headed out the door, carrying my shit, to my new place of residence. In prison, you are free to move around within certain guidelines because you aren't going anywhere. Guard towers surround the entire place. Plus, where you gonna run to? Another one of the six neighboring prisons?

Fuck.

When I got to my "barn" I noticed it was a cluster of four pods. These weren't pods like I'd seen before, though. This was a giant dayroom with bunk beds lined up along the walls and showers dead in the center of the room, right under the TVs.

That meant every time I wanted to watch TV, I had to see naked dudes in the shower. Fuck...Fuck...Fuckity...Fuck.

I put my shit on my bed and waited, figuring at any minute some dude was going to come over and test me. I would have to fight immediately. Everyone was staring at me.

Nobody said shit.

I was one of the only white guys in the pod. Of probably 300 people, there were 50 who were Mexican and the rest were black. It was a fucking awkward time for me. C-Pain and his crew were always nice to me, sort of. But I made them money. These guys hated white people. In their mind, white people locked them up. White cops, white judge, white narcs, etc.

I made my bunk and laid down to go to sleep. Then I passed out until about three in the morning.

This "Gurney Unit" was a transfer facility. Inmates came and went every day. It was like a bus station for prisoners.

When 3am rolled around, it was time for breakfast. I thought *fuck this is early*, but went and ate anyway. Due to the car wash and being the sales guy who never got a break, I was used to eating quickly and on the run. I also knew you couldn't share food in prison.

We piled in the chow hall and filled each table in the order that we got our food. By the time all the tables filled up, the first table had to get up and the rest followed suit. Again, it was a bad ass assembly line to feed 5,000 inmates in three hours.

The rule was no talking in the chow hall. You barely had time to eat, let alone strike up a conversation.

When we went back to the barn, I started asking questions of one of the inmates who was awake on his bunk next to mine. I wanted to know how it worked. He went on to tell me, but in a quiet voice.

I just assumed everyone there was like me. New. Turned out. That was not the case. Some of the men in the pod had lived there for a couple years and worked all night. As one of them was trying to sleep a few bunks over, I was being loud next to him and asking questions.

After a couple of minutes and without warning, the inmate, a black dude, jumped up and started yelling at me. He wasn't that big, so I said some smart-ass shit back to him.

Big or not, fucker could fight.

I mean, I thought I could fight him, but this dude was handy as fuck. He'd spent his fair share of times in this exact same situation and he was getting a chance to prove his handy work again. Some dudes love to fight for no reason at all. I'm not one of them, but this dude was.

He didn't kill me, but he definitely killed my pride and ego. The rest of the 298 inmates in the barn laughed at me. The white guys all said, "You gonna let that nigger do you that way? You better stab him if you want any backing from us." The black dudes said, "Fucking white boys are all pussies."

Two days later, I got a layin' and transferred to another barn about 500 yards down the strip. Same prison, just a different part. Word spreads quickly in prison, though. They had all heard about me already.

Over the next two weeks, I fought two more black dudes. Won one, lost the other. My lightweight ass was on them pushups and workouts every day after that. I needed to get big to make it in there.

A couple weeks later, I was on the chain again to another prison, this time I thought it would be a permanent home, which they call a "farm."

I was sent to this big-ass prison somewhere in Texas. It was old as hell, had three tiers of cells and held about 300 people in each wing. A violent motherfucker.

The worst part, was the fact that it was like you see in the movies, where everyone showers together. I hated that I had seen it all. It fucking sucks to hear, let alone see. It was crazy. I spent about four months in this place in what was supposedly the low security part where the good guys are housed.

After four months, I was transferred to a prison in downtown Dallas. Can't remember the name of it, but it is right smack dab in downtown Dallas in a high rise. I lived on floor seven or some shit.

This place was a "Wackenhut" facility, and my first lesson in how corrupt our government is. Not only was I doing time for $200 worth of drugs, costing them thousands a day to hold me, they subcontracted the prisons out to a company which is publicly traded on Wall Street.

It's the modern day transatlantic slave trade. These fuckers make money off of inmates. There are more black males incarcerated in private prisons than there ever were as slaves in America. Chew on that shit.

I stayed at that prison in Dallas for a couple months; fought a few times, got a tattoo and even convinced some of my friends to visit me and bring cash and drugs. It was bad food-wise, but wide the fuck open to smoke weed and chill all day.

Remember that gun and weed charge I got when I was going hunting? Well it came back to haunt me. The constable came to the prison in Dallas and took me back on a bench warrant to Collin County to face court.

I spent probably three months in county, went to court, pled guilty, got time served and was sent back to Gurney. This time in the barn, in the dead of summer, with no air conditioning—there's none in Texas prisons—it was a musty motherfucker.

It was there I would finish my sentence out and make parole just a few months before my 24-month term was up. So much for my lawyer and his "four months and you'll be home on parole" speech. Fuck that guy.

Chapter 14: Time to Go Home

The last couple months before my release were a nightmare. I went home sometime in early 2002. I don't exactly remember the date because I had gotten accustomed to not looking at calendars or clocks. I just existed.

For most of my time spent locked up, I was dead sober. I'd smoked a few joints while I was incarcerated, but not a lot. I'd moved around so much it was hard to gain anyone's trust.

I ate the same, farm fresh food for the most part and lived the cleanest life I'd ever lived to that point. My mind was clear. I didn't need time or days; I just existed, like I said. A dog in a cage who's occasionally let in the backyard, just existing and awake.

Looking back on it, I had some pretty deep thoughts for a 21-year old.

I quickly figured out that no matter how much money you could make selling drugs, the risk was too high to balance the reward.

Prison is full of men who've sold lots of drugs and made lots of money. Some of these guys got caught with hundreds or thousands of dollars in cash. Some with millions in drug contraband.

No matter how much money, drugs, women, cars, houses or anything else these men had had at one time, it was all gone now. Everything they had worked for their entire lives was gone. They had been reduced to living in a barn without air conditioning or nice things.

Even the dudes who are lucky enough to have money on their books for commissary can only buy ice cream. Yeah, there may be overpriced, diluted drugs for sale in prison, but it is not the same. No matter how rich you are, if you gain it illegally, it can go a million times faster than it came.

Because of this little revelation at 22 years old, I vowed never to sell drugs ever again. Never. No matter what.

A few months before I was to leave, I got a bullshit night job in the kitchen. Man it sucked. I had to cook two meals a day for 6,000 inmates. Some dudes liked the job because they got to eat. Fuck that, I was gonna eat anyway. I didn't want to cook.

This is prison we are talking about here, so it's not like I had a choice. I'd go in about 11pm and cook food until 67am—seven-hour shifts sweating over a grill or stove, cooking for twelve thousand.

Fuck, it sucked!!!

One morning, after preparing meals and ending my duty in the kitchen, I went back to my dorm room and the fucking water was off. Well, it wasn't off, it was brown.

In other words, the water was out. Dammit. I was sweaty, stinky, tired and irritable as fuck. Now I couldn't even take a shower and pass out. My OCD wouldn't let me. I had to wait it out.

One of the dudes came over to me and started talking about some shit. I wasn't in a mood to hear it, so I told him to fuck off and leave me alone. We ended up talking more shit and got into a fistfight.

I got the best of him until the very last shot when I had him backed against a cinder block wall and was laying it on him left, right, left, right, uppercut, elbow... I was giving it to him and fucking him up, taking out six months of aggression.

I reared back with my right hand in a "finishing move" gesture and went to knock his fucking head in. When I swung he fell down unconscious before I connected.

It was too late to stop my swing and I hit the cinder block wall full force. Destroyed my right hand, the same right hand I had already fucked up jumping out the window, running from my stepdad.

He was fucked up. I was fucked up and the guards rushed in to see what all the action was about. We denied doing anything and even though our blood was everywhere, they didn't feel like doing paperwork, so they left it alone.

After the fight, it was about 10am and I looked up at the TVs. All the inmates, even the guards were staring. The news had interrupted and shown some smoking buildings with planes hanging out of them.

I thought it was a commercial for some crazy movie or something. Then I quickly realized it was NYC and this was some real shit going down. It was September 11, 2001.

I sat there, hand hurting, body sore, stinking like shit, tired as fuck and locked up. Yet, I felt sorry for the thousands of people who were experiencing, or about to experience, such terror.

When the buildings fell, you could hear a pin drop inside the entire prison. A moment of silence wasn't asked for; it was mandatory.

In prison, you find some of the best-behaved people you will ever meet. Not because they want to act right, but because they are afraid to get the shit stomped out of them if they disrespect someone.

Kind of how it works in Texas. Everyone here for the most part is pretty polite compared to a lot of places I have been. I think it is because in Texas everyone has a gun.

You stay on your behavior, so you don't get shot.

The next few days around the compound were different. Dudes were nicer. People seemed to think a little more before they did stuff. It was just different.

A month or so down the road, the president announced we were going to war with terror. Bush said he would not stop until it was gone from the planet.

Some of the guys got all paranoid and thought back to WW2 when they locked up and killed off all the Japanese. We were prisoners; we were enemies of the state. If they went to war, we could all be killed, drafted, or both.

Riots ensued for weeks. Not like any riot ever lasted for weeks, but they would riot for like two days, get locked down for five days, then be back at it after getting all rested up.

It kept me up at night; it made me paranoid. At the same time, it was inmates versus guards, so the camaraderie was kind of cool. After a while though, it got old. There was no way for those guys to win anyway. If they did win, what did they want? It's not like the guards were going to let them out.

One night, I was sent to the other end of the unit. When I got there, I was given the option to make a phone call. I had no one to call, so I didn't make one.

The next day, I was called out to "go home." I was on the chain to Huntsville, Texas where all the inmates in Texas are dispatched from the system.

I packed my shit and at 3am when it was nice and quiet, I screamed out loud, "I'm going home, bitches!!!! You fuckers are nuts. I hope many of you never get out of this place. Most of you fuckers belong here!!" I was happy to leave it all behind when it was my turn to go.

The bus ride to Huntsville was rough. We made a lot of stops and it was a long route. When I got to Huntsville, they let me call my mom. I left her a voice message telling her I would be home the next day.

In the morning, I got up, gave all my shit away and went to the Walls Unit to leave prison. The Walls

Unit is old as dirt. It's an intimidating prison from the outside, but beautiful inside. Hard to explain, I know, but trust me.

When it was my turn to leave, the paperwork didn't come. Some mistake had happened with my other cases and they needed time to sort them out. I got all hyped up for nothing. To make matters worse, they were shipping me back to the first unit where I'd just yelled at everyone.

The universe was looking out for me, though. I didn't go back to the barn; I went to some prerelease wing where no one knew me. Talk about relief... Fuck.

A month later, they would call my name again and I would repeat the entire process, minus the yelling, plus actually getting out.

I was free, and with a whole new perspective on life. I hadn't yet begun to live my legit, legal, normal, productive citizen's existence.

Chapter 15: Working at the Car Wash—Again

My mom picked me up from the Greyhound station in downtown Dallas. She seemed genuinely glad to see me. It makes sense she was happy, I was sober and alive for the first time in years. I had definitely learned my lesson.

While I'd been locked up, my mom and stepdad had sold their home and built a new house on the west side of town. When I left to go to prison, the neighborhood they lived in hadn't even existed yet.

I remember clear as a bell, what happened that first night.

When my mom and I got to the house, my stepdad and sister were waiting on me. We had a nice dinner, talked, laughed and caught up.

After my sister, who was like 13 at the time, went to bed, my stepdad asked to have a talk with me.

He went on to tell me that I could live in his house for a few months as long as I minded some rules.

1. No girls in the house
2. No drugs in the house
3. No friends over
4. I had to have a job

5. I had to save money

He also said he would put me to work at the car wash again. If I acted right and did my job well, I could become manager one day.

With a felony on my record, it didn't sound like a bad gig. After all, my stepdad had made about $90K in his position at the car wash for the past 20 years. I would take over for him one day.

I took him up on the job and quickly fell into a routine. I would wake up at 5am, go to the gym with my stepdad and then he would drop me off at the car wash each morning.

I lived at home, so my stepdad and I would argue a lot over dumb shit. I had to walk on fucking eggshells at work *and* at home. It was tearing down my nerves on a daily basis.

At the time I didn't know it, but my stepdad was really into steroids. Had I known, a lot more shit would have made sense.

I remember talking to my pal, Brandon when I was around 13 years old. I had just seen a commercial in school for alcoholic parents. The signs were short fuse, temper, angry, violent, etc.

I told Brandon, "Man, there is not a drop of alcohol in my entire house, but I swear my stepdad has all the signs of an alcoholic." Brandon thought I was just angry at my folks and dismissed it.

At the ripe age of 12 or so, I had no clue about steroids, but later in life I would learn the signs of alcoholism mirror the effects of steroids.

When I was locked up, I worked out seven days a week. I'd do 1,000 push-ups, 1,000 sit-ups and run every single day. My stepdad had always been a big and strong dude. At the height of his time, he could half squat like 600 pounds. I always thought he was just some cock-strong redneck.

Anyways, he offered to work out with me first thing in the mornings before dropping me off at the car wash. I had no car and the bus didn't run to Allen, so I took him up on his offer. We started working out at 5am Monday through Friday.

He introduced me to his gym buddies and we had a pretty good thing going. One day, he asked me if I had ever run across steroids or juice in my drug days. Honestly, I hadn't. My clients had been junkies and stoners, not the steroid type.

He told me he had a hook up and if I wanted to bulk up he'd buy a round for us. In retrospect, I guess it was his way of roping me into his world. I would be a prime candidate to get addicted. Of course, I took him up on it.

Eventually, I found a good hook up and I would score for us both. Here I was, a dude on parole, doing steroids and living at home. Total douchebag move. He was my boss, my dad and all I had, so to me it seemed normal. I'm not playing victim; I'm just telling you how it was.

We got along well, though. I worked hard for him, got the car wash location to number two and eventually got a car. I moved out after about two months. I had a car and a place to live. I also had a job with a steroid addiction.

Six months into my release, my stepdad got a call that his father had passed away. My stepdad not only adopted me, he was adopted, too. That means I come from a long line of fucked up families, I guess. His birth father had died shortly before, as well. In one year, he'd lost both of his fathers.

One of those two, not sure which, had been in the Korean War or some shit. At least that's the story I get. For all I know, that was 100 percent complete bullshit. Because he'd been in the war, he got to keep his fully automatic rifle. It was badass and shot .308s, intimidating as fuck.

When my stepdad had inherited the full auto version of whatever gun it was, he wanted to sell the semi-auto version he already owned. This was way before social media and Craigslist. You had to sell guns to someone you knew.

Pops wanted $1,000 for the gun and nobody he knew carried that type of cash. He asked me if any of my drug dealer pals might be interested. Again, at the time, I thought this was totally normal. After all, it was my dad asking me to do this shit.

I called around and found a friend of a friend who said they would buy the gun. I loaded the gun in my car (felony) and took it over to an apartment in Dallas. The dude met me in the garage where he had a safe. When he opened it, it was full of money, guns and meth. I liked to shit my pants.

Got the cash; got the fuck outta there and got out. Then I went home to put a plan together to get the fuck out of this life. I needed to keep Pops happy, but at the same time I didn't want to keep it up with the steroids, guns and felonies. I got out, and I wanted to stay out.

I had worked at the car wash for about a year when I finally got my own store. It was in Plano. We had a regular customer who would come in each week. Her name was Monica. She always made me upsell her—I think she kinda got off on it.

Truth told, until I reached about 33, I had no clue what female buying signs were. I had no idea if a chick liked me or what. It's a wonder how I ever got laid.

Monica asked me one day, "Why do you work for this car wash? You're a hell of a salesman, why don't you get a real job? Hell, come work for me. I'll teach you to do mortgages."

I told her, "Lady, I'm a convicted felon. I don't even have a credit card, let alone a mortgage. Thanks, but no thanks."

She chuckled to herself and drove on into the car wash area.

The next week, and the week after that, she and I repeated the conversation. And so on...

Turned out, Monica had a really good eye for talent— diamond in the rough type of talent— which is a weird coincidence since she happened to be a diamond broker.

At the time this was going on, I was married. Yes, married. I didn't talk about it much because it only lasted six months and took place in a courthouse. Much like military guys coming home and falling in love with the first piece of pussy they get, the same thing happens to convicts.

She was encouraging me to get the fuck out of the car wash business and make some real money. We fought night and day. I didn't believe in myself. I identified myself as a felon, a convict and a failure who had no choice but to wash cars. She saw my talent, which is probably why she married me.

Some days the planets just line up...

It was a rainy day, and the car wash was about to close. The owner came in and started demanding that we do odd jobs around the place. You could tell he was drunk, hung over and had been in a pissing match with his wife all night. He came to our spot to stir the pot.

I was too young to understand the psychology of self-destructive men at the time, but this was it. I fell right into the trap and my mouth and his shot back and forth. I threw my keys at him and quit. Then picked my keys up and took the car wash keys off and chucked them again!

I wasn't on parole at the time, so I had no worries. I was a free man.

I called Monica, who told me to get to her office, dressed for work the following day. That's exactly what I did.

Chapter 16: Oh You're in Real Estate Now?

I walked in to that office in what I thought was my best set of clothes. I looked like a fucking ass clown. The worst part was that this was not some class act brokerage either. I looked like a jerk off even in a room full of amateurs.

At the time, I had no idea what "cut your teeth" or any of those other similar corporate terms meant. I just knew I had bills to pay, no income, no job at the car wash and all the desire in the world to make shit happen. I was down to learn. The problem was no one had time to teach me.

I remember going home to wife number one, and her asking me what took place on my first day at work. I told her all I'd done was sit around. Honestly, I was worried. I'd never had a commission-only job. I had no clue what a 1099 versus a W2 was. All I knew was I didn't get paid unless I sold something, and I didn't even know what a mortgage was or how to sell it.

That didn't stop me from going back on day two. Day two is clear as a bell to me, still. I was in Monica's office, leaning over her shoulder watching her work on a computer. At the time, I had never really used a computer. I was unfamiliar with the Internet; I had a lot more to learn than just mortgages.

As I sat there, in jeans and boots, watching over the shoulder of my new boss, a dude walked in and started talking about his commission numbers. He had made like $40K in the past month. That was what I used to make in a year! My mind was fucking blown.

I'd been taught by my stepdad to judge a dude by his size. I was still a good size from the steroids, and I had spent my time working manual labor jobs. Jobs where you picked a guy for his physical size and strength, not his brain.

The dude who was throwing numbers around like they were lightweight kettle bells, was tall, thin and something didn't feel right to me about him. After he left, I asked Monica what the deal was with his huge lion head belt buckle. She told me the lion was the brand for Versace and that it was an expensive belt. She also said, "Gay guys are such fancy dressers."

It took me a minute. "That dude is gay?" I asked her and I'm sure it was obvious to everyone else, but the only gay dudes I'd ever seen had been in prison and on television. Come to think about it, I didn't know shit about how the world worked. I wonder how many people never get a chance to learn things outside their box.

I didn't give a shit if he was gay, straight, or a fucking alien. I wanted this dude to teach me how in the hell he'd made $40K in the last month. So, I followed him into his office, introduced myself to him and to the two other people who were there. Apparently, they were there to learn from him, too. They had both just started and were relying on him to give them deals. I was even more impressed. I knew this was the dude who could show me how to make some serious money.

I asked him if he would let me observe how they did loans and learn from him. He agreed and showed me to a seat where I could check out the three of them doing what they did best…printing money!

Of the two people who worked for Claude (the gay dude), one of them was a guy who looked like he could play football for the Dallas Cowboys as a starting linebacker. He was about 6' 2", 260 pounds and in phenomenal shape. I was taught in prison and by my stepdad to always make friends with the big guy. That's exactly what I did.

The big dude's name was Drez. He was actually Claude's roommate. This struck me as odd at the time. Claude was the first openly gay dude I had ever met, let alone befriended. Drez was his roommate. In my mind that meant Drez was gay, too, and it boggled me. Drez could have had any chick he wanted, so what was he doing with a dude? In my trips to West Hollywood in the future, I would learn there are lots of good looking, cut gay dudes.

Turned out, Drez was not gay. He was fresh out of federal prison for a drug conspiracy and Claude was his long-term friend who'd given him a place to stay. To this day, Drez is still my very best friend. I made a bud for life within a couple of weeks in my new job. You'll hear killer stories of our shenanigans as this story continues.

I didn't have any money yet. I needed money bad. My wife was bitching at me, shit was upside down at home and I was starving. Every day though, the people from the mortgage office would meet at a place called The Rover and have drinks. I could never afford to join them, so I would stay in the office learning from Claude or researching my own shit. I wanted to go, too, I just couldn't afford it.

My First Check

When my first week on the job was over, I had the day off. I was used to working Saturdays at the car wash, so it was weird to have free time. I went over to my long-time homeboy Rick's house to watch

Ohio State play football. (His family is from Ohio and they are super fans). I'd known Rick since seventh grade, and his parents have watched me do some straight up retarded shit.

For example, Rick's last name is Johnson. In the late 90's his parents bought a fancy-ass door knocker for their front door with "Johnson" inscribed on it. They were super proud of that thing. About a week after they got it, we took a screwdriver and inscribed "Magic" above "Johnson." They were pretty bent out of shape on that one!

These are the types of shithead moves I was known for.

I remember this clearly. You never forget your first big check—that first deal and how it went down. I was sitting on their couch cheering for Ohio, even though I have no clue about college football. We were having a few beers and Rick's mom asked me what I was doing for work. One thing they knew about me was that I always had a job. Even if it was selling rocks or working in prison, they knew I was a worker.

I told them I had just left the car wash and got a job in the mortgage business. Then it hit me. I asked them how long they had lived in their home; I suspected at least 10 years. They told me they had lived there for 14 years, and had built it new.

I asked them if they had ever done a refinance. They told me they hadn't. So, I asked a few more questions and before you know it, told them I would have my broker contact them, then ended with, "I think I can save you money."

The following Monday, I went into work with a mission. I told the broker I needed the application to take to my friend's house. She gave me the app and a checklist of shit to get from the Johnson's. After work that day, I headed right over to their home.

I was honest from the jump with the Johnson's, told them I had no clue how it worked. If they would fill out this paperwork, I'd take it to my broker and get them some numbers. They went along with it and I did what I said I was going to do, took the app back to the office.

Monica, my broker, was pumped. She was excited that I had no experience, but already had an application in week one. She helped me put the loan package together and after work, I headed back to the Johnson's to discuss terms. Monica loaded my lips with exactly what to say. She was a bad ass mentor.

The Johnson's were ecstatic with the terms. It would cut their loan time, save them monthly cash and even get them $2,500 back in time for Christmas shopping. It was a winwin situation for us all—especially me. But I had no idea what I was in for the next day when I brought the signed app back.

Monica took the signed loan docs from me and told me to watch how she put it all together. I tried to take in every detail. When she finished, she looked at me and said, "Your cut of this deal is $6,300." I said, "You mean like thousands?" She smiled and said, "Yeah, thousands, car wash guy."

I had just made in one week at my new job, what would have taken me three months to earn at the car wash. Holy fucking, fuckity fuck, I was on cloud nine!

I got a call two days later from the landscaper guy who mowed the yards at the car wash. He said he had heard I was in the mortgage business. This landscaper was also a dude who worked out in the gym with my dad and me each morning. He knew me well. He said he was buying a home and wanted me to do the loan.

It was a $770,000 home he was buying! To put it in perspective, the Johnson's home was a $160,000 loan.

This was going to be an epic portion of money.

I closed these two loans in one month and made almost $20,000 in that time period. Stupidly rich for a car wash guy. I couldn't believe it. My parents were still pissed that I had quit the car wash. I'm 100 percent sure they thought I was selling drugs again.

In less than 40 days, I had bought a new truck and a new house and filled it with furniture paid for in cash. No credit card debt. If there was one thing I'd learned from the dope game, it was to stay debt-free 'cause you never want to owe money. Avoid that shit at all costs.

Spoiler alert: I climbed the ranks quickly at the mortgage brokerage.

Chapter 17: Meth, Money and Mathematics

Claude liked my work, so much so, that he gave me my third loan. A dude named Walt White. I shit you not. It was 2003, or 2004, so pre-*Breaking Bad*, but I was about to break bad in my own little way.

The first time I'd left prison, I'd promised myself I wouldn't ever sell drugs again. I'm proud to say that as of 2015, I've still kept that promise to myself. However, I never promised not to do them.

I hadn't touched weed, meth, coke, or anything else since before I went to prison. I'd had my fair share of drunken nights, but I just wasn't willing to risk using drugs. They were offered to me all the time, but much like these days I politely declined. Thing is, nobody ever gave, or gives me shit for it.

Most of the time when someone would offer me weed or some kind of drug, I would think to myself *Is this person more successful than I am?"* I've found that 99 percent of people who have asked me to do drugs had a lot less to lose than I did.

I'd always had this picture in my head of how the corporate world would look. Suits, ties and straight edge people. The first week or so on the job at the mortgage brokerage, made me realize corporate folks were just like car wash people in a lot of ways. They just had more money and fancier things.

Everyone likes to drink, party and have a good time no matter where they work.

At the car wash, there were plenty of dudes who didn't do drugs. I never found myself hanging with them. I'd always gravitated towards the drug users. It felt like I fit in easier with them. In the corporate world, there were people who didn't do drugs, too. I found myself quickly surrounded by the ones who did partake.

A few weeks into the job we had a race to see who could drop off 100 door hangars the quickest. We all met in a neighborhood and each had a partner and 50 door hangars.

My partner was Raylon. Raylon had a Dodge truck with a 12-inch lift on it. It was a ridiculously, fucking huge machine to have in the city. The redneck in me loved it! We Texans love our big-ass trucks and this one was enormous.

Raylon and I ran door-to-door dropping off these hangers—ads for refinancing people's mortgages. Monica had picked the perfect priced and aged neighborhood for us to farm. She was a brilliant bitch.

The first team to drop all the hangers and meet back at the parking point got $100 and lunch at a local steakhouse. Raylon and I beat second place by about 15 minutes. We won that shit and at the time, I needed $50 in cash like you couldn't believe.

We got our cash, hopped in Raylon's monster truck and headed over to the steakhouse to meet Monica and the rest of the staff. It was one in the afternoon. I rode with Raylon to save on gas money. I had loans closing at the time, but it would be another week or two before I got the first big check. So, I was piss broke.

When I got in Raylon's truck to leave the office, I noticed he had one of those DWI breath things. I'd seen a lot of them, so it wasn't a big deal. Much like everyone else who has one in their car, he felt the need to tell me the story behind it.

Apparently, he had been a cop in Austin, Texas. His chick broke up with him, he got drunk, got in a fight, then got arrested leaving the scene of the fight. Typical story, nothing big.

When we got to the steakhouse, I noticed everyone had drinks. It was early in the afternoon and I thought we were going back to work. I'd never drank on the job before. What in the fuck? I loved the corporate world. Well, at least the one I lived in. Turns out, it wasn't so corporate, after all.

I ordered a beer. The boss was there, and she was buying. We ate great food and had a shit ton of drinks. I was definitely buzzed when we left. As we were about to leave, I noticed Raylon having two more shots of whiskey. I wondered how in the fuck he was going to crank his truck.

He stopped by the bar on his way out the door and ordered a pink lemonade. I remembered him asking if they had any when we'd gotten there, but then ordering a beer instead. I didn't think anything of it. Right before we headed out, he grabbed the pink lemonade and started out the door to his monster truck.

I struggled to jump in the motherfucker, but Raylon had it down pat. He got in, turned his key, picked up the breath device, took a swig of the drink, held the device to his lips, and gargled the pink lemonade while blowing into the device. Unbelievably, it beeped and the truck started! He looked at me and said, "Little trick I learned when I was a cop." I was impressed.

When we got back to the office, a dude named Kayson was there. I had heard about him from Claude. Kayson was the go-to guy, handsome, a smooth talker; he had banged pretty much every chick on the floor of the office.

Raylon introduced me to Kayson and we instantly became friends. Kayson was getting a divorce and was kind of down on his luck. So, still pretty drunk, I headed to Fort Worth to party with Kayson. Half-ass drunk, I was like, "Man let's party, fuck problems." And he was down like four flat tires. At 5:30pm I hopped in his ride and we left Frisco to head to Fort Worth. To party.

I didn't bother to call or let my wife know I wouldn't be coming home any time soon. Occasionally, she stripped for cash, so I had the night to do whatever the fuck I wanted.

We got to Fort Worth and arrived at a place kind of in the country. Everyone at the house was high as giraffe pussy. They didn't call their drug of choice meth, though. Instead, they called it ice to make it sound classier.

The kind of people at this house were different as fuck to me. I was used to seeing poor people on drugs, but these were successful folks. A lead singer for a popular local rock band, a motocross winner and several fine chicks were there. I thought I was in a good spot.

After a few more beers, I started talking to one of the chicks. She asked if I had ever tried ice and offered me some. Of course, I smoked it. In about 15 minutes, I, too was high as giraffe pussy.

Speaking of pussy, all I could think about was hers. I didn't hit it though. I was still married.

Kayson and I kicked it at the party until about one-thirty in the morning. Then Kayson took me back to the office and dropped me off, so I could get home before my wife got back from the strip club. He gave me a Xanax, Viagra and about $50 worth of ice for free. He called it a party pack. We told each other we'd had a good time and parted ways.

When I got home, my wife was already there. She also had a girlfriend with her from the club. They were in the bathtub together. I was high out of my mind, had a Viagra and two hot chicks ready to do whatever the fuck I wanted. Game on.

I must have fucked the two of them for four hours before they'd had enough. This ice shit was amazing and the Viagra was the frosting on the cake. I didn't tell my wife I had drugs. She must have thought I was just really happy to be in my first (and only, so far) three way.

To put it lightly, that experience on ice was one of the most amazing feelings ever. However, I'd spend the next six months trying to find that same high and I'd lose everything to get it.

Chapter 18: Bad Business

After the Walter White file closed and funded, I had a good grip of money. I paid off my bills and invested in a couple of flip homes. About four months later, they had made me about $10,000 each and I was getting pretty good at doing what I did.

I was also making more contacts in the builder world because of my mortgage experience. So, I was making money, momentum and massive changes in my world.

Things were on the up and up.

One night, I had Brant over to my new house. He was intrigued at all the nice shit I had, then went on to start bitching about his job as an electrician and how fucking hot it was. I told him I could get him a job with me. Brant is a Grade A ass kisser. Employers love him because he makes a great employee.

He met with Monica a few days later and made the shift to be my partner. Brant's dad had a lot of old-timer friends. Brant planned to hit them up and teach them how to invest in real estate. Some of them still sold weed, so this was a good place for them to hide some cash.

I worked night and day to get Brant up to speed on how the mortgage game worked. We would spend 10+ hours a day in the office and then go home to my place and watch investor training programs I had bought from seminars.

Soon, Brant was able to hit me up with his first client. An old redneck, mechanic, dirt bag idiot named Rob. Rob was as dumb as they come. Which is exactly why that shiesty fuck, Brant took advantage of him.

Allow me to paint a picture of Rob. In his early 50's, he looked seventy and had definitely endured a hard life and done plenty of hard drugs. He dipped, too, so he always had a nasty ass ring of dried chew spit in the corners of his mouth. A person best kept out of public places.

When I was younger, I used to believe anyone could be successful and that it didn't take a lot of work or skill. As a young man, I had no clue about what a $30,000 millionaire meant. When people looked successful to me, I assumed it was what it was. Years of mortgage applications would change my way of thinking.

Rob and Brant were not bright people. Rob had been on his job for 20 years—barely any raises— and steady work at a Dodge dealership working on transmissions. He made about $70K a year and his wife had been semi-smart with it.

Employers love guys like Rob. Hell, like I said earlier, they loved Brant, too. Both men took direction well and didn't think out of the box too much. They also weren't that intelligent, so they couldn't steal company info. The likelihood they would become competition was nonexistent.

Truth is, lenders love guys like Rob, too. He'd had the same job for a long time, steady income and all the documents he needed to get pretty much whatever amount of mortgage money he wanted in 2004.

I wasn't in the business of turning down money, so I took Rob on as a client…the very first loan Brant had sent my way.

I wanted to make an example out of Rob. If I could make him rich, I could prove any dumb-ass could make money in real estate. I searched for the perfect home for about a month without luck. Then Rob came to me one day and told me I needed to meet his friend Reggie.

Rob gave me Reggie's number and told me to call him. Turned out, Reggie worked for the largest lender in the USA in the REO department. In layman's terms, this guy controlled foreclosed real estate inventory. I could get deals from him for way below market price!

Reggie agreed to meet me in two days for drinks to discuss opportunities and strategies. The meeting place: On The Border. The bribe he wanted: hydrocodone pills.

I told Rob that Reggie had asked me for pills and it wasn't my thing. Rob told me to relax, said he took like 30+ pills a day and had been doing so for the last three or four years. He told me he had a hookup and would get me the pills I needed.

I met Reggie at OTB and we had some margaritas and talked about certain properties and my expectations. He told me about his job description and love for pills.

After a few drinks, I got a call from one of my homeboys who happened to be in the area. Brant had also called wanting to meet up. I told them where I was and to come over.

We got pretty smashed up after OTB that night, and we decided to call Kayson and head to Fort Worth to get some "ice." At 10pm we got "the urge." I called Kayson and asked what was up in Fort Worth. As you know, that meant: "Where's the ice?"

Reggie, Brant, Tom and I all piled in my 2003 Dodge 4door truck and headed to some motel off Meacham Blvd. in Fort Worth. I was four or five margaritas into it; Reggie had a pocket full of about 60 pills and I was flying down the highway.

Soon, I saw a cop turn his lights on behind me. I thought, *Fuck, last thing I need is a DWI. This Reggie guy has all the pills, if I need to, I'll get him to take the charge and the DWI won't even be on the plate.* There was no way I was going back to jail.

As I was pulling over my truck to the shoulder on the service road, Reggie started flipping out. He said, "Man, I got a good job, a wife, kids. I can't go to jail, man. I can't hold these pills."

He was yelling at the top of his lungs. I felt like the cop, who hadn't even gotten out of his car yet, could hear him, which made me severely pissed. This corporate pussy was about to get me in trouble. So, I went into survival mode.

As did Tom. He'd had enough of Reggie's incessant yelling. Tom was in the back, Reggie in the passenger seat. From the back seat, Tom took Reggie's seat belt and wrapped it around his neck.

He said, "Listen, you, corporate pussy fuck. Shut the fuck up. Don't yell and let Ryan handle this. If anything happens to us, I will kill you and your family."

To be clear, Tom is not a gangster and has no criminal record. He was just saying the right words to freeze the situation because I knew I was a salesman and could probably talk my way into only getting a speeding ticket.

Tom eased the belt from around Reggie's neck, and the redness in Reggie's face faded back to white right before the cop showed up to my window.

"License and registration, please," the cop said.

"Here you go, sir." I gave my stuff to him.

"Where you boys headed tonight? Have you had anything to drink?"

"We're headed to Fort Worth to meet up with some girls. That's the reason I was speeding. We do crazy stuff for women. And no sir, we planned on drinking once we got to our destination." I told him in a cool manner.

He wrote me a speeding ticket and let me go. No further questions, no issues at all.

A normal person would have turned around and called it a night after that close call. Not me. I already had this dude pegged as a pill head, so I thought, *let's see how he does around ice. I'll get all my properties at cost forever.* Reggie fit in at the hotel party like a whore in church. He didn't look, talk, or act like any of us. But I was determined to get him iced up, so I could get the best real estate deals on the planet.

The dark side of Ryan was out that night.

He was some corporate pussy who had never lived life.

We were all living it.

There were a couple of THOTs at the gig who were all iced up and ready to fuck anyone. I got Reggie high and laid. Now, I should have been a shoo-in for the best real estate deals on the planet.

I was also becoming addicted to meth.

Chapter 19: Badder Business

The following Monday, I put in an offer on a home with Reggie. He gave me the bottom dollar the bank would take for the property, just like he promised. From what I remember, the house was foreclosed on, had been empty and had about 90K worth of equity.

Brant got Rob a loan for the price of the home. I was already divorced and needed a place to live, so I agreed to live in the house and rent it out until someone bought it. This was a 4,700 square foot home, and we got our hands on it for $190,000, even though it was worth around $280,000.

Being a single dude in a huge house with no kids made for hella good times.

I had a party damn near every weekend. I always kept my promise not to sell drugs, but I introduced a few people to JD, the main dealer guy. However, I did my fair share of ice, there's no denying that.

For the first month or so, I partied a lot and stayed up all night just getting high. After I got bored with that, I stopped going out and started skitzing out on a business plan.

I remember numerous times when Kayson or Brant would show up at 2am, iced out of their mind, trying to party, and would end up mad at me because I wouldn't stop working. I became obsessed with real estate and numbers. I had a meth-fueled addiction to information.

About six months into the ice bender, I finished my business plan. It was a foolproof strategy to flip 30 homes per month. I had all the details worked out from earnest money to rental income. This plan was the shit.

Like anything else I've done, I took action and followed my plan exactly. I also had a serious drug routine by now.

I'd wake up each day around five in the morning, eat, brush my teeth, shower and do a line of ice. I'd work all day and do one more line after I forced myself to eat lunch. By 4pm I'd swallow a Xanax and be able to come down and sleep by eleven.

I got in the habit of always wearing dark glasses, so prospects couldn't see my eyes. I was a mess, no doubt about it. At the same time, when people heard and saw my plan, they knew it was the best they had ever seen. They knew I was high as fuck, but also that I was brilliant. So, they were willing to overlook my drug problem.

Rob wanted in on the action from my plan and so did Brant. All three of us partnered up into an LLC and started what would be the biggest lesson and the worst business experience I would ever have.
But before I go into that, let me tell you how wife number two came about.

Second Wife

Wife number one left me in a whirr one day. She'd had enough of my using drugs and wanted to get her 3-year old daughter away from me. Not that I ever hurt or even yelled at her kid, it just wasn't a safe environment and honestly, it was a smart move.

One thing wife number one did to contribute to my life was encourage me to call Monica. She believed in me and even stripped to pay bills while I got started in the mortgage business. When she left, she took everything— every dollar in the account—and all the furniture.

But she left me with a newfound confidence and a bad ass career.

One night, I had a party at my house. JD was there, as was the singer from a popular local band, as well as the tour bus belonging to that band, that was parked out in front of my home…in the street…in a subdivision.

It was only there for two days before the HOA and neighbors made them leave, but those two days were epic!

Imagine iced out groupies naked everywhere, and any drug you want, right there and free. All the pussy and drugs you could want for two days straight. Motherfuckers were going nonstop.

We weren't selling drugs. We were celebrating with drugs. People would come over and share with us. It was nuts— full blown nuts.

On day two, this hot blonde shows up and gets iced out and naked quick. Every dude in the house, even JD, tried to hit that. She was a 19-year old blonde firecracker.

Country girl, too with one of those southern drawls.

After a couple of hours of drugs and me running game, I got her in my room, but when I went to fuck her, the damned meth + GHB combo killed my drive. I was tripping because I had a hot chick in front of me, horny as hell, yet my dick was paralyzed.

Of course, I had other ways of making it worth her time, but I didn't want her to leave the next day UNTIL I got a chance to hit that. HARD.

She stayed over all night, and the next morning I had to go to Grapevine to pay that damned ticket I'd gotten when Reggie had flipped out in my truck. I talked her into riding with me to the courthouse. Our first date…court.

She was not dressed appropriately to be going into the courtroom, so I asked her to wait for me. I went in, paid my shit ticket and came back to the truck. From the start of our first date, we were joined at the hip. We went back to my house and it was empty, so we fucked for 24 hours straight and after that, were pretty much inseparable.

Wife number two was 20 and I was 26 when we got married. She was a loyal and down-ass chick, also young, blonde and smoking hot. She started working with me in the real estate business and after taking the test six times, got her license.

We spent our days riding around meeting builder reps inspecting inventory. This was all part of my plan. If we had to deal with a male sales rep, she'd do the talking. If it was a lady, I'd do it. We had about 10 builders selling us lowball priced inventory.

We were taking those properties and selling them to Brant's investors and Rob's friends. I was making a killing.

An absolute killing.

We sold so many houses, had so many investors and made so much cash, I couldn't count it all. I was pulling in a month, what I used to make at the car wash in five years. My life had dramatically changed. This was at the height of the subprime mortgage boom. Money was everywhere, thanks to George W. Bush.

Part of my plan involved property management, too. Once a home had been bought, I'd get the rent. I wasn't even doing loans anymore. Brant, Rob and I were just flipping homes.

One of the investors was Rob's mom. Another investor was Brant's dad's best friend. We worked solely on referrals. Although, we did have one outsider I'd met at an investor seminar, Don.

Don told us he was an ex-Navy Seal. He was always strapped and one weird fuck. He'd had his whole face cut off and it was sewn back on. You could see the scar around his entire head. I asked him a few times what happened, but he refused to talk about it.

Don basically forced me to sell him a home. He was an intimidating motherfucker. In the end, I think he was the only smart one to make a profit from our venture. I made sure of it. I didn't want that fucker to come after me.

Rob's mom and Brant's dad's homey each bought five or six houses. They made a killing in cash, but had trouble getting them rented. Being the nice guy I am, I offered to help them get renters. I wanted us all to be successful. I'd soon learn success wasn't for everyone.

My office was in Allen and I used to stay there all night working. It drove wife number two crazy, and after the plan worked she begged me to quit ice. I did. Just like that. Put it down for two months and then one night I relapsed, but only a little.

She found out about it and left me. I guess even though we met while high, she had become not cool with it. We decided to take a month break.

Towards the end of that break, I went on a date with some Asian chick who was friends with Rob. Rob insisted I go out with her even though I've never really been attracted to Asians. (No offense, they are just not my type).

While on the date, I was trying to be cool and when she asked me what I did for a living, I replied, "I rob banks with real estate." I'd had a few drinks by this time and was just being a big douche talking shit to impress myself. She was totally not feeling it.

The date ended without a goodnight kiss or anything. I never thought nothing of it. When Rob asked me about her, I told him she wasn't my type. No big deal, on to the next one.

About three days later, Future Wife #2 (FW2) called and wanted to meet up. Funny thing about human minds and decisions. Once you've made a decision on someone, it's hard to change your mind. She missed me and wanted to visit. I wanted to get laid!

I agreed to meet up with her the following morning to ride around, look at new builders together and talk.

That night, I planned on going to the concert of the band I mentioned earlier. The concert was awesome. I went on the tour bus, got stoned as hell and then ended up doing ice. FML!!! FW2 was gonna kill me.

Fuck It.

I called JD and he came and delivered some good cold ice to us at the venue.

This band was rowdy. All the members I knew are now dead, if that tells you anything. They were known for fighting and fucking dudes' chicks and giving them STDs.

Not exactly stand up gentlemen.

After the concert, they initiated a big fight and goddamned, a riot happened. The lead singer got his nose broken and it was all I could do to make it out of there. Three o'clock in the morning in Dallas in the middle of a 30-person fight is no place for a real estate entrepreneur.

I called JD and went to get "just a little more" to take the edge off.

After I'd taken the last bit, FW2 hit me up on my cell phone.

She left a message saying she was naked in my bed. Fuck, I couldn't go home. I was high as shit. She would lose it.

I couldn't stay at JD's, or I'd keep getting high. This relapse was gonna kill me.

So, cruising the streets of downtown Dallas in my truck, I ignored my girlfriend's calls and turned my phone off. Really, I was wasting time, trying to come down from the high before I went home.

As I cruised down the road, I got to a stop light to see a young dude freeze right where he'd been walking in the street and fall down. With parked cars on both sides of me, dude had me blocked in on a one lane, one-way road.

I got out and he told me he was drugged and needed a ride two blocks over. We were in uptown Dallas and this was like some SMU kid. Not a street bum. I helped him into my truck and he passed out.

Three minutes later, he woke up, snapped out of it and started attacking me while I was driving. I realized he was out of his mind. In retrospect, he probably came to and thought I was some gay dude about to rape him or some shit. Regardless, he was hitting me and I had to end that.

I grabbed the knife out of the side pocket in my truck and I stabbed the dude in the shoulder, then twisted the handle.

When he jerked back, I flung his door open and kicked him out going 20 MPH.

All that "ice" wore off quickly when the adrenaline faded. I was stone cold sober and covered in blood, so I hit the car wash before sunup and got my shit cleaned up.

Then I drove back to Allen, borrowed my stepdad's big-ass truck, loaded FW2 up, Brant and his chick up and we drove to New Orleans to party. I wanted to get the fuck out of town in case the SMU kid wound up on the news.

We partied it up in New Orleans. And I never told anyone until later about the incident. Everyone just assumed I was in a festive mood. Little did I know, my life was about to take an unexpected hit—a shit storm that would be waiting for me in Texas.

Chapter 20: The Raid

When we got back from NOLA, my business credit card was frozen. Rob usually handled that, so I called him to see what gave. He was nowhere to be found. No returned calls, nothing. I had no other card on me, but thank God I had cash to get us home.

Turns out, the chick Rob had insisted I go on a date with, came back to him and told him I was a bank robber and he would be in big trouble if he got caught up with me.

Just like that, no questions asked, Rob's dumb-ass went to the FBI. They must have looked at him like a retarded cow when he called them and then showed up telling his story.

Luckily, they didn't take him seriously.

First off, nothing I did was illegal. I only told the date that because I was buzzed and trying to be a cool bad boy type.

Second, Rob had no clue how anything we did worked. He only lent the credit and cash to get started. His job was to pay bills and introduce us to new investors. That's as far as his duties went. He could only speculate WTF we were actually doing.

Regardless, Rob kicked me out of the house he owned from our first deal, and I had to move ASAP. Rob was a pill-poppin' nutcase. He was no doubt capable of coming over and shooting me, a felon in a house he owned.

About a month prior, I had sold my parents a new home. They'd had their current home on the market and I offered to rent it from them. Since they needed help covering the bills for two homes, it was a win- win.

I moved in almost overnight. This time Brant and FW2 moved in with me. Brant took the upstairs and I took the master bedroom downstairs. This house was nicer than the other one and it had a pool. Game on.

A few months before we all moved in, I had paid for a cruise for two, to join the rest of my family. My birth father, grandparents and other various family members had signed up for a five-day trip to Mexico.

Not long after I moved into my parent's home in Twin Creeks, it was time to go to Mexico. I had to drive to Galveston, Texas and then get on the boat. FW2 was with me.

We hauled ass down the freeway and stayed overnight in a hotel to make sure we didn't miss the boat the next morning. We loaded up on time without a hitch. This would be only the third time I had ever left the country, and it was also my first cruise.

(I did manage to have a run-in with the Mexican cops while in Cozumel, at a private beach, but I bought my way out of that one pretty easily. FW2 was nervous, but I had it under control).

After the cruise ended, I hopped in my truck and headed back to Allen with FW2. We stopped off in Dallas to grab a check from one of the brokers who owed me about $3,500.

It wasn't much, but with my card still cut off, I needed cash.

I showed up to the house in Allen with $3,500 in my visor and a joint in my ashtray we had partially smoked on the way from Dallas to Allen.

As I pulled down Wills Point Drive, I saw several trucks and cars in my driveway and what appeared to be an ambulance, too. I thought to myself that Rob must've killed Brant, and started sweating.

As I got closer to the house, I realized it was not an ambulance, but a SWAT team vehicle. The fucking Allen cops were in my house raiding it!

I wasn't sure what to think, so as I got closer I turned off to the right, and a cop with an M16 was on that street and recognized me. He pulled me over, hit me on the head with the butt of the gun and dragged FW2 out by her shoulders.

Both of us went from vacation mode to lying on the ground at 3pm in the middle of my street with neighbors and kids watching us raided like criminals. I was all too familiar with this shit. So I knew I hadn't done anything wrong.

I immediately yelled, "We didn't hurt anybody! Is Brant alive?"

The cop looked puzzled. I thought they were there because Brant was dead, but it turns out they'd come on a drug warrant. A drug warrant? What in the actual fuck had gone down while I was gone?

As the cop read us our rights and escorted us in the home, I saw the damage from the flash bomb they had thrown in my house. The door was never locked!! Dammit! My carpet and stairs were burnt the fuck up.

I also saw Brant. Sitting there with cuffs on just like we had. They separated us and yelled during our interviews, which a cop on a computer recorded.

I was pissed!

"Drugs? I don't have any drugs, you fucking idiots. This warrant says you are here for a meth lab. You threw a flash bomb in a meth lab? You're all idiots. Second of all, my lawyer's gonna run over you. There are no drugs here." I was telling the truth, but where had they gotten their information? I had never sold drugs since I had taken that pledge to myself. I've never run a meth lab. How the hell did they get this intel? "Fucking Rob!" I was unaware, but Rob had told them lies to buy time to steal some money from us after the FBI had told him to fuck off.

I didn't even know he had talked to the FBI. I had no clue how in the hell the cops thought I had a meth lab since I didn't even have foil or bags in my house, let alone drugs.

They did, however, find a Glock .357 caliber pistol that belonged to my stepdad. He had given it and a SIG 9mm to Brant and I for helping us get him the new house. Why he chose to give us guns, I'll never know.

Regardless, I had the gun and about 100 rounds of ammo. It was five years after my offense date, so in Texas, I could have a gun in my home again. The only thing I was thinking was that I was gonna kill this case and sue the shit out of the Allen PD for the damage to my house.

They arrested me for felon in possession of firearm, and misdemeanor possession of weed, for the roach in my truck. *What a fucking joke*, I thought. Thirty thousand dollars of your tax money went to a roach and a perfectly legal unused handgun. *Good work, Allen.*

They let Brant and FW2 out on bail after three hours. I, on the other hand, didn't get out for three days. They seriously thought I had been out of the country doing a drug run or some shit. For the life of them, they couldn't figure out how I had come up legally, and was living well. Haters.

The "reason" I couldn't bail out, was the FBI had a damned hold on me. What in the actual fuck was the FBI involved in? You know how it is. I started thinking back to any wrong thing I had ever done in my life. All the way down to stealing cookies from mom as a toddler.

The FBI arrived three days later and called me up, in handcuffs, to this office way above the jail in the new police building. It was one of those rooms with the double-sided mirrors. Just like CSI and shit. I had been to prison and was a former felon, but had never seen one of those.

A special agent walked in and slammed papers down on the table. He said, "We got you, you might as well just start spitting out the details of how you did it."

"Did what?" I inquired.

"I've got pictures of you using stolen credit cards taken from an IP address at 504 Audubon in McKinney. These are credit cards you currently own. Here's the pictures of you on camera."

It wasn't me; it was one of my rental home tenants. Apparently, this sneaky fuck turned the Internet on in my name and stole credit cards from the Internet, also in my name. Man, was I pissed!

I took the agents over to my rental house and they handled business from there. I've never been one to snitch, but trying to fuck me over is never a good idea. They took me back to the station, lifted the FBI hold and let me bail out on the gun and weed charge.

FW2 came to pick me up that night, and I could tell she was as happy as a cat in a bathtub. I just wanted to know how in the hell all of this had happened while I was on vacation. And she was likely thinking the same thing, so I understood exactly how she felt. And I was determined to find out what had taken place and who had done this to me.

The first person I asked was Brant. Then I kicked him out of my house because I didn't believe a word he told me. I knew he had to have done something and my guess was that it involved my money and Rob.

Chapter 21: Neighbors from Hell

I can imagine living next door to a home that was just raided by the cops, especially if I were a parent, which I am now. Seeing all those cops in the house, asking them what's going on and the cops saying, "We are here to bust a meth lab," would probably cause me to hate my neighbors, too.

As you can guess, that was the situation. My neighbors hated me. None of them ever asked for my side of the story, and they must have all made some kind of pact to get me the fuck out of the neighborhood.

I was out on bond, and trying to take my mind off of the situation, when I decided to throw a small party and invite some of my clients and referral partners over. I only invited like maybe 20 people and planned on just drinking, talking and chillin' poolside.

Those 20 people turned into about fifty, which is no big deal to me because they all brought weed and drank. No one was fighting, no drugs were dealt and no crazy shit was going down. Just some young successful people having a good time on a Friday night.

My next door neighbors weren't trying to hear it.

I can only guess the cops must have given the neighbors their contact info and told them to holler if anything happened. I'm sure those coward-ass cops thought I was slick enough to hide the drugs. They would never have believed I was legit, no matter how much I proved it to them.

At about 11pm, the cops showed up. They started asking to come in. I yelled back, "Get a warrant, you fucking pig!" while I was at the door. I fucking hate cops and all they stand for. Show me a good one, I'll show you 100 crooked ones. Police, preachers and politicians are 97 percent scammers

The cops tried all sorts of shit to get me to end my party. Problem was, I wasn't loud, didn't have drugs and was 100 percent within my rights. As you well know, cops don't like it when you point out they are violating your rights. When that happens, they feel it's their duty to lie to you in order to fuck you over.

Think about undercover cops. These guys are the biggest pieces of shit on the planet. They make people feel they are friends, lie to them, assume a fake identity and after getting to know and befriending a suspect for years, the undercover cop turns on them and throws them in jail. If that ain't the most fucked up personality trait on the planet, I don't know what is.

What I am trying to tell you is that in my experience I've found that many cops lie—a lot. Matter of fact, 99 percent of the shit cops say are lies to get you to confess to something. Cops are 100 percent always working an angle... *Anything you say CAN and WILL be used AGAINST you.*

So, after arguing for a while, the cops decided there was no way to arrest me for anything and left. I shut the party down and called it a night.

A couple weeks later, I closed a big deal and invited 10 of my friends over for drinks and a smoke. We were all sitting in the backyard by the pool talking, when I heard the doorbell.

I went to answer the door, and saw it was the fucking cops again. Jeezus!! Can I not get some sort of break from these oppressive assholes?

Again, they wanted to come in and search my house. One thing is for sure, these dumb fucks were persistent in asking to illegally search my shit. At this point, the 10 of us were not loud, not obnoxious and just chillin' poolside. My neighbors were calling the cops every time someone came to my house. Those pieces of shit.

One night, when I was drunk, I banged on my neighbor's door. When I became really violent, I got him to confess he had been calling the cops on me as instructed. I wanted to kill this motherfucker. Instead, I made a big decision about how I would handle him in a flash second.

I moved!

That's right. Without warning to anyone, I moved across town. To turn the knife on my bitch neighbor, I made sure the yard was never mowed. The whole time the house was on the market, I never once cut the grass. Hopefully, the mosquitos would fuck him up every time he went outside.

I was facing prison again, had lost my dream home, cops were following me everywhere and I couldn't take it. The pressure was just too much. I went into "fuck it mode" and stopped paying bills on rental homes as I started stacking cash to fight my cases.

The house I moved to was rented and I didn't update my license, so the cops had no idea where I'd moved. I even went as far as to get new cars for me and FW2, so we didn't get harassed driving down the street.

In retrospect, I don't know why I didn't move to Dallas. I have no clue why I stayed in Allen. That fucked city had cost me school, jail and would soon cost me my freedom.

Yet, like a fucking idiot, I stayed.

The new house was smaller and low-key. None of the neighbors knew of me or my situation. Cops never came over; neighbors were cool and after a while, life seemed to get back on track.

I had cleaned up. Gotten rid of fake friends, gotten off meth, quit smoking weed and even landed a corporate job as a loan officer with a really good brokerage. I was doing my absolute best to live the straightest life I could.

Chapter 22: BOOM, BOOM! Open the door! ATF!

I had been at my new loan officer job for a total of a week when I got a call.

The call went something like this:

"Mr. Stewman?"

"Yes this is Ryan. How can I help you?"

"It's special agent, Meade. I've got my hands on a Glock 17 that you had back in 2000. Turns out, the gun was stolen. I'm gonna need you to come down here and answer some questions. I'm at the Bank of America building off 75 and Park in Plano. When can you be here?"

"What the fuck? That gun has been in police custody since late 1999 or 2000. You're in a bank building? Is this some kind of prank call? If I drive over there and you are fucking with me, you will regret it. I've got a job to do, and no time for fucking games."

"Mr. Stewman I assure you this is no game. Can you be here by 5pm today?"

"I'm on my way now."

I still remember it. I was mad as fuck and scared at the same damn time. When I'd been pulled over and arrested for the gun and the weed, the gun had been taken away and not given back. To this day, I couldn't tell you who I'd bought the gun from or anything about it. The fact that it might have been stolen from a cop scared the fuck out of me. *Was it a dead cop*?

I got in my truck and drove over to the bank building, which was only 15 minutes away. I was thinking hard about everything I'd ever done in my life on the way there, scouring the depths of my mind trying to figure out where I'd gotten that pistol.

I was also so fucking mad at myself that I thought about driving off the bridge twice.

There I was, brand new dream job, first day on that dream job and headed to most likely be arrested for some bullshit I couldn't prove I hadn't done. I wasn't sure exactly what I'd done in a past life to deserve the one I'd been living, but I was pissed nonetheless.

I had worked so hard up to this point. Shaken drug addictions, fought to have a real job, lived life by the rules. Hell, I had even started going to church. That 15-minute ride to the B of A building was full of nothing but negative thoughts.

When I arrived at the building, I called the number from my phone as I stood by the elevators. Within a couple of minutes two ATF officers came out of the elevator.

"You Ryan?" The one on the right asked.

Before I could even finish nodding my head, the one on the left pulled out cuffs. I knew the drill, so I turned around, hands behind my back and surrendered. The officer latched the cuffs on me, then took me by the shoulder and escorted me to their car.

Once I got inside the car, they started talking to me about the situation. I knew it was going to be a long car ride. I had been arrested in Plano and the federal holding facility was in Sherman. Basically, we were driving from Dallas to Oklahoma.

I asked if I could make a few calls. The first call was to my stepdad. He knew all my passwords and had a key to my house. I hadn't told FW2 anything yet. I also knew that my stepdad's neighbor was a higher-up in the Plano PD, so I asked stepdad to call the cop and ask what was going on.

The shit you see on cop television is fake. These guys never read me my rights, never told me what I was charged for and totally lied to me to get me to show up at their office because they were too lazy to drive to pick me up. Fucking cocksucking cops...

Turns out, the charges had nothing to do with the gun I had back in 2000. They were over the police raid in my house in Allen. I had beat the state case due to a statute of limitations. However, federally there were no limitations. I had been double jeopardy'd. There is no double jeopardy when it comes to state and fed. That's when I found out our government is full of dirty tricks and workarounds.

I arrived at the federal holding facility and was booked. After formally being charged with "Felon in possession of a firearm," I met a prerelease officer who said the following, "If you pass this piss test you go home. If you fail it, you will not get a bond. Ever. Before you take it, have you done any drugs lately?'

I just grabbed the cup and pulled my dick out to piss. I've never failed a drug test. My metabolism is so high nothing stays in my system more than a day or so. Luckily, I hadn't smoked weed for months. My test came back clean as a whistle.

I had arrived at the jailhouse too late to speak to a judge over my bond that day, but I was promised to get a bond hearing the next morning. That meant spending another night in jail, something I'd promised myself I'd never do again.

After I passed the piss test, I was sent to a jail bunker that held about five other inmates. I told them my charges and that I should be gone the next day. They laughed and told me the cops said that to everybody. All of these dudes had been here over a month and they had not seen a single person go home after their bond hearing.

"FUCK MY LIFE!!!!!!"

I was ANGRY! I screamed with fury over circumstances, deities, friends, myself and everything I could think of. *How the fuck does a guy live a straight-laced life and end up back in prison on some BS, wrong double jeopardy charges?*

Let's think about how shady and fucking crooked cops are. They lie to you for a living, take everything you say and try to figure out if they can arrest or cite you for it. They harass you and if you beat them in court, they will retaliate against you to make sure it doesn't happen again. Undercover cops are worse. They act like they are friends with people in order to eventually destroy their lives and put them in prison. Fuck cops. Each year more people are arrested by cops than there are people helped by cops. Chew on that.

The cops in my city had thought they'd caught a big time drug dealer. They lied to get the warrant, lied about what they'd found in my house and when I beat them in court, they lied to the Feds and got me arrested. The Allen cops testified on paper I had traveled over two states with the gun, but it had never left my drawer since it had been in my possession.

The next morning, I was called out and escorted to the bond hearing. When I arrived in the court booth to see the judge via live satellite, I saw my lawyer and FW2 sitting behind me. Thank God, they were there to get me out. My lawyer was good, he'd beaten the case once, and he was there to rescue me from this injustice.

He did just that. Got me out with no bond and released within two hours. When I went back to the jailhouse to retrieve my shit, the other inmates were amazed. One of them even said I was a snitch. "There's no way anyone leaves here on a gun charge without being a snitch." That wasn't true, because I had no one to snitch on. I'd lived a clean life and my case only had one suspect. Me.

At least I was out, free and able to try and save myself.

The sad part was, my life was about to get even worse.

Chapter 23: Fuck It, I'm Out

When I say, "I was out free," I use the term lightly. I was under heavy scrutiny. This is your tax money at work, people. I had to call a phone line each day, enter my PIN and see if I had to take a random drug test. I took about three tests a week. If I were gonna waste the taxpayer's money, I'd do it with drug tests.

Federal pre-trial release or not, I had a lot of responsibilities and shit to do. I helped manage about 37 properties I had sold to my investors. Most of them were rented out without any issues, with good tenants in them.

Notice I said "most"?

A home in Rockwall, Texas, a small-ass town east of Dallas, was the exception. Rockwall County is one of the smallest counties in Texas. It's a lake community with nice homes ranging from $250,000 to $10,000,000.

In Rockwall, ten million bucks will get you 100 acres, and 40,000 square foot mansions with barns and animals to go along with them (for tax exemption purposes, of course). All sorts of beautiful homes are lined up along the shores of Lake Ray Hubbard.

In 2005, Rockwall was booming. My grandpa used to own a glass plant there in the 80's, so when I came across an opportunity to invest there, I jumped on it. Normally, I wouldn't buy or recommend a $280,000 rental home to my investors. At the time, the market was not there. Buying a home for $180,000 or less made sense according to market conditions.

Long story short, I got one of my investors to buy the home from me. I flipped the Rockwall home with the promise to get it rented out on behalf of the investor.

I found this renter who was a TV executive for a local Spanish channel. Seemed like a good fit and he had the cash down payment and income to afford the rent. We signed the contract and he moved in. I had officially rented out the big-ass house. Mission accomplished.

After about three months, the guy stopped paying rent. I made a million attempts to call, text, email and everything else I could do to get ahold of him. Finally, I knew I had to make a trip out there to see if I could talk to the tenant myself, eviction notice in hand.

When I knocked on the door, he opened it and served me with bankruptcy papers. Motherfucker! This meant I couldn't collect his owed rent, too. It was October 2005, the new bankruptcy laws had gone into effect in November, and the courts were backed up for months. This guy got a free ride and free rent for three months. It wound up costing me $10,000 plus attorney fees just to kick the dude out. All my effort and shit had been wasted, and I lost money on the home.

The investors I had gotten from Brant and Rob were now starting to bitch and moan about renters and other shit that you're supposed to take care of. Rob and Brant had hit the bricks and left me as the only one trying to hold my word.

I'm always the one left trying to do right. I've seen so many people just walk away and not give a fuck who they hurt. I can't do it. If I give my word, I do my damnedest to make shit happen. People know this about me and sometimes will use it against me.

Rob's mom was one of those people. She had bought five houses from our company and when Rob split, he took the money we collected for her with him. I'd assumed he was taking care of his mom's deals, but he wasn't.

She was furious and going broke. Like any other mother, she refused to blame her son and instead sought legal counsel. She sued me, Brant, the bank, the title company, the appraiser and everyone who touched the house. She hired a frivolous lawyer who smelled blood.

I showed up at home after getting the bankruptcy papers from the tenant to only then be served by a processor for the lawsuit filed by Rob's mom, Carlita.

So let's get this straight...

...I'm out on federal pre-trial release. I've been served bankruptcy papers by the most expensive tenant I manage, and I get served with a million-dollar lawsuit and am 100%, completely flat broke. Between lawyers, unrented properties and partners stealing from me, I had nothing. I didn't tell anyone, but I definitely lost years of my life and months of sleep over it.

I remember living in a $400,000 house and scraping up quarters with FW2 in order to go get food from the dollar menu for dinner. I refused to sell or pawn anything. I'd always figure out a way to make things happen. It was getting harder though.

I was killing myself. My health was deteriorating and I was only in my mid-twenties. I couldn't use pot to cope because I was on random drug testing. Luckily, I still had a job because the bank hadn't fired me. And I'd never told them about any of what had occurred.

Then one day I just quit. I moved out of my home into a cheaper spot to rent, sold my racecar and got a 4-door Nissan. I told my investors, who I hadn't originated directly, to deal with Brant and Rob for their money, and I decided to stop trying to please everyone and instead focus on me.

I got 100 percent centered on doing loans and put all of my efforts into my W2 loan officer job. I used all my knowledge as an investor to get loans from people who wanted investment property. Like a group out of Beverly Hills who would send me 10-15 deals a month with great credit and 20 percent down. That was a loan officer's dream come true.

Best part was that all I had to do was the loan, and they handled the rest. I was almost stress-free. The workload kept me so busy I didn't have time to think about the federal prison I would soon occupy.

After six months of being sober and focused on loans, I was at the top of my game. The number one agent in Dallas sent me all of his referrals and I had a huge pool of investors relying on me for money. I was making $30-$50K per month W2 money while on federal pre-trial release.

I had saved up six figures in post-taxed money. FW2 and I were really on a roll. She was a processor at the same bank and we stacked paper together like I had never done before. All my bills and debts were paid and I had cash.

Eventually, I settled the lawsuit, but not after a lot of time and money wasted. Shit was starting to clear up, and I was getting back on track. If I could just get probation from the Feds, I'd be good to go. With court coming up, I'd soon find out.

A month before my final court date with the Feds, my lawyer got elected as the first democratic black district attorney in Dallas County. He won the election with a $3,000 budget against a white guy who had a million-plus budget.

I asked him how he did it, and he said, "There are more black folks in south Dallas than there are rich white folks in the north. The minority community knows how to work the system and vote, all I had to do was get them out of the house to actually vote. We bussed them all in. Meanwhile, the white folks up north just assumed their guy won and didn't vote."

Dude was smart as shit—took the metroplex by surprise. But he couldn't represent me anymore. This would both work in my favor and against me at the same time.

Chapter 24: Court Date

The Feds were not happy a black democrat had won the election, and they offered me 25 years since he represented me. I was literally watching politics play out in front of my eyes, with my life being the pawn.

I refused to sign papers for 25 years. I'd rather take my chance in court. That's exactly what I told my lawyer, too. Twenty-five years was the max anyway, so I had nothing to lose. My lawyer felt bad for me because it was a tough time.

I remember being so mad at God that I didn't know what to do. I had been tithing, living right, minding the rules and here I was, facing 25 fucking years. If that was an all-forgiving God, fuck him. One thing was for sure, I'd gotten myself into this situation. I was gonna get myself out, even if that meant doing the time.

It was about four weeks from my court date when I met with my attorney for the last time. He explained he couldn't represent me any longer since he'd taken the DA position. He did hook me up and introduced me to his friend, though, a senator from south Dallas, who was an attorney.

The senator told my lawyer he would take care of me and see that I got proper representation. As soon as my lawyer left the room, the senator tried to get me to plead out to the 25 years. Fucking crooked-ass, lazy fucking politician. I was angry!

The senator then turned me over to his subordinate. I'd had three lawyers in less than a day. The new lawyer told me to hop in his Escalade and take a ride to the courthouse, so we could file something. On the way to the courthouse in Sherman from south Dallas, I told him the story.

When we went to court that day, he called me by the wrong name in front of the judge. I thought my life was over. Seriously, who had I fucked over to end up like this? I wanted to kill myself because I felt like such a victim.

When the DA was my lawyer, I'd done some favors for him to help ease my legal fees. I refinanced his house, helped his wife get a car, sent them title business and anything else I could do to contribute financially to them. He liked me and he hadn't given up on me.

About a week before my court date, Dallas caught some dudes who had robbed a half dozen or so banks. The Feds wanted the suspects, but Dallas wanted them, too. It was a big power struggle between the state and the Feds. My DA lawyer was at the forefront of it all—bucking the system, just like he promised in his campaign.

When push came to shove and shit hit the fan, he used me as a bargaining chip. He traded the robbers for me and a handful of guys to get reduced sentences. No sniffing, no BS, just less time. He came through and delivered!

I got a plea agreement for 15 months in minimum security federal prison. They even sent me to a prison close to Dallas. I would sign the papers and all in about three days.

I knew I was going to prison long before I was sentenced. At the first mention of 25 years, I had a feeling I was in serious trouble. This was my second offense and they weren't kidding. This was the third time I had gotten busted with a gun, so I was definitely a threat in their eyes.

Knowing this and knowing how the game goes, I turned FW2 into W2 in October of the previous year. We ran off to Vegas with her sister and dad and got married at the Little White Wedding Chapel. I gave her control of my assets, a signed power of attorney and added her to my bank account.

She seemed like someone I could trust to hold shit down for a year while I was gone. She worked at the same place I did, so all I needed to do was teach her to do loans and she could even run my business while I was gone. I'd come out without missing a beat.

I went to court that week, stood up in front of a judge who didn't know me, an ADA who hated me and a courtroom full of people who served the government not the people. It was way worse than when I had faced court the first time. This time, I had shit to lose. I had lived a clean life and done right, and this was painful.

I broke into tears.

I knew I only had to do 15 months, but it was a lot on my plate. My new lawyer stood up in the court and addressed the judge and he literally called me Mr. Spillmen, I was so glad I had already signed papers.

The judge was nice enough to give me 60 days to get my affairs in order. I was to drive to FCI Seagoville on Friday June 15, 2007 and turn myself in. From there I would do 13.5 of 15 months. Behind bars. Again.

I had 60 days to get my entire life in order and try not to stress about it every second of every day. It was as if that judge had put a weight on my back that grew exponentially heavier every day that passed.

I couldn't tell my clients or referral partners I was going to prison. I was too embarrassed to tell the people in church what was going on, so I lived a fake life for 60 days.

I also went into "fuck it" mode. I stopped showing up to take drug tests, started smoking weed and drinking pretty heavily. One of the other loan officers where I worked had a boat. I spent several days a week trying to wakeboard behind it.

Meanwhile W2 was learning how to originate loans and beginning to understand a little about it. She wasn't that bright, so it took a lot of patience on my end. I knew I had no choice; all my money was bet on this horse. I had to see it through to the end of the race.

I had houses, cash, furniture, stocks and other assets worth hundreds of thousands of dollars I needed to leave her with; she was my only bet. My only chance of someone supporting me while I was gone. I trusted her 100 percent.

Chapter 25: The Worst Day of My Life

The last week before I had to turn myself in was horrible. A fucking nightmare. The story I'm about to share with you is mind blowing. I'm not one to play the victim, but I can't make this shit up.

Life can do some fucked up shit to us humans. I'm about to reveal the worst situation I've ever been in, in my entire life. Only someone you love can hurt you this bad. This is the EXACT reason it's hard for us humans to fall in love and trust someone.

*****

I had to turn myself into FCI Seagoville on June 15, 2007. It was a Friday, in the middle of the hot-ass summer. I remember the state pen not having air conditioning, and I was not looking forward to my fate. Even trying to dull it all by smoking weed, I could no longer hide the fact shit was getting real.

On June 12, 2007 it was a Wednesday and also my stepdad's birthday. My mom, sister, stepdad, W2 and me all met at Steve Field's steak house in Plano for a birthday/going to prison family get-together.

While at the steakhouse, we had a solid family talk. Good times. I had only one drink—Jack on the rocks—along with a steak and lobster meal. It was a great experience and made me realize how much I was going to miss everyone.

After dinner, we said our goodbyes and all agreed to meet up and ride together to drop me off at prison in two days. W2 and I hopped into the Nissan Altima and headed north to our home in Allen.

Somewhere along the way, I decided I wanted to get high. W2 smoked weed pretty regularly and her brother was the dude who hooked her up all the time. I called him on my Nextel flip phone and the conversation went something like this:

"Hey man, you know I only got two days until I leave. I need a small favor. Can you bring me a bag of weed? I'll pay you for the bag. I just don't want to run the risk of driving with drugs right this minute"

"I don't know man. I wasn't planning on getting out tonight."

"What? Dude, I've paid your rent, done a million favors for you and I leave for prison in two days. You can't do me one last solid?"

"Like I said, man I wasn't planning on getting out. You can come by here though, if you want."

"Naw man, fuck it..." *Click*

I was steaming hot, sitting in the passenger side of the Altima. W2 was driving and heard the conversation. After I hung up I said:

"Can you believe that piece of shit lazy fuck?"

"Don't call my brother names."

"Fuck him, he should have jumped out of his way to help me. Lord knows, I've helped him a ton."

"You know what? I told you not to say another word about my brother. I'm taking you to your parent's house. I don't want to listen to this shit tonight."

"My parents' house? WTF for? If anything, you need to go somewhere. I own the house we live in and have, long before you were my wife."

"That's it. I'm taking you to your parents."

"Dude, it's my dad's birthday. He's probably fucking my mom right now. NO. You take me home."

She made the left turn to go to my folks' house instead of the right turn to go to our home. When she got to the next light and started to slow down, I pulled an old school gangster trick I had practiced in case the mafia ever kidnapped me.

From the passenger seat, I popped the middle gear shift into neutral. She could hardly figure out what was going on before it was too late.

I then took the middle e-brake and slowly raised it. At the same time, I reached over with my right hand and grabbed the wheel, then I steered us to a stop just inside an empty parking lot.

She was screaming at the top of her lungs, fuming mad. I can't blame her. Imagine how pissed you would be if a passenger in your car commandeered and riskily drove you to a screeching halt.

I have no recollection of what she was hollering, but it was starting to piss me off. I hopped in the driver's side of the car and she began to walk. It was around 9:30pm, so the streets weren't busy, but they weren't empty either.

I wasn't mad at her. I understood the dynamics of what was going on. Well, so I thought. I figured we were both frustrated I was leaving. Turns out, she had a plan.

When I pulled up next to her, I begged her to get in. After a few trial closes, she reluctantly agreed. Then she went to yelling again, but I'd had enough.

"Listen, you fucking cunt. Shut the fuck up before I leave you jobless, broke and fucking alone. I'm in no mood to hear this shit anymore tonight. I gotta go to fucking prison in 36 hours... FUCK!!!"

About the time the last, hard "K" noise came out, she had reached back and punched me twice in the eye before I could blink. Turns out, she packed a hell of a punch and wound up hitting me harder than most guys ever had. My eye swelled up immediately.

"Ho-lee fuck. You fucking white trash cunt. What the fuck are you thinking?" I said as I grabbed her hand, tight as fuck, to ensure that shit didn't happen again. I wanted to knock her the fuck out, but (A) I don't hit chicks and (B) she clocked me with damn near as much force as I have. I didn't want to get my ass kicked.

An eerie silence during the 5-minute car ride from the incident to the house fell over us. I pulled into the driveway, opened the garage and parked the car. I went in the house first, changed into comfortable clothes, then headed into the backyard to puff a cigar.

In an unreal move, she grabbed her phone, went in the bedroom and called the cops. She told them I'd beaten her up and they came to her aid.

I was in the back yard when the door opened. It was the cops asking me to step outside. They asked what had happened. With my eye black and my face swollen, I told them the story.

They arrested me for domestic violence because she had a red mark on her arm. When I asked about my face, they said it was self-defense. Fucking punk-ass cops. I guess they thought they had a shot at fucking being heroes to my girl. Turned out, she pressed charges first and they'd had no choice.

I was going to jail, 30 hours before I had to drive myself to prison. Please kill me now!

We got to the Allen city jail around 10pm. After I was booked in, I fell asleep. They woke me up at 1am and transported me to Collin County jail. At 8am, I had a bond hearing with a magistrate.

The judge informed me that I had a restraining order and could not go to my home or within 500 feet of my wife. I was fucking shocked and felt like I had been set up.

By the time I got to the bank, my money had been cashed out. I couldn't go to my house and I couldn't even get a shower or toothbrush. I had to borrow money from a friend to bail me out, and I couldn't pay him back. She took over $50,000 in cash in less than 10 hours.

I was fucked. All my hard work and plans were gone. My wife gone and my freedom gone. I went to my parents' house to chill for the night, and they'd take me to prison the next day. *Fuck it. I'll just stay in.*

About 8pm, my wife called. She begged me to meet up with her. Like a fool, I did. All she tried to do was convince me as to why she'd done what she had and that she loved me. She got me to sign a power of attorney. I'm such a fucking idiot. It wouldn't be long before she sold and cashed out my entire stock portfolio on E-trade.

My ass was starting to get sore from all the people fucking me in it.

Chapter 26: Club Fed

That Friday, I woke up and ate breakfast with my mom and stepdad. I had stayed at their house the night before. When I had met W2 that previous night, I had been so pissed and hurt I didn't even wanna fuck her.

Here I am, about to go 15 months without pussy and I'm so disgusted by this bitch I wouldn't even let her suck my dick. I was torn. I had power of attorneys and all the stuff drawn up and no time to change it. W2 was an evil bitch and she was about to control my entire net worth.

At 2pm, my parents, W2, my sister and I all rode to Seagoville, Texas, so I could turn myself in to the federal prison system. I was broken, beaten by W2 and wanted to die, but I had to get mentally tough to pull off what was about to happen.

Once I entered the prison yard, all the shit that had happened to me wouldn't matter. I had to get my head on straight.

Unfortunately/fortunately, I was all too familiar with this shit. I knew when I got inside those prison doors, the suit-wearing church guy had to kick rocks, and the old "Stewman" had to show up.

I had to be ready to fight and protect myself at all times.

When I said goodbye to my family and walked in the doors, the guards were there waiting for me. I went through the take-in process and eventually, was sent to my dorm.

After entering the prison facility from the FDC side and letting them take my blood, my DNA and check me in, they let me out the back door and I walked over to the FCI part of the prison.

FCI Seagoville is as old as fuck. It's a massive compound of red brick buildings with no air conditioning and about 3,000 inmates. On one hand, it was a beautiful compound and had it been a college campus, I would have loved it. On the other hand, it had an eerie feeling of confinement.

I was assigned to Building C, so I made my way over to the back of the property and went up in to the day room, where I would find my bed next to 10 others. Two-man cells had been set up in the building, but everyone had to start out in the day room.

I looked around the day room at my new roommates. In the corner bunk sat a 400-pound Mexican dude with tattoos all over his face and body. I thought to myself, *that's a fuck ton of ink.*

My bunk mate was this big-ass black dude who looked about as thrilled to see me share his post as he must have been when he got sentenced. Fuck! I hate prisoners.

I hadn't been hunched on my bottom bunk for five minutes when in walked Dave. Dave was about 6' 3" and bald, covered in tattoos and looking mean as hell. I thought to myself, *this is it, this is the guy who's gonna check you, Ryan. Be ready.*

Dave walked up and said, "Hey man, I got you some soap, toothbrush and other stuff you'll need while you're here."

I told him, "It's all good, man. I don't need your stuff. I'll just wait for store day."

I knew if I took the stuff from him, it would be bad news. I hadn't been on the compound for 15 minutes and they were trying to get me in debt to them. I knew the hustles because I had been in before, knew if this dude loaned me "supplies" and I didn't pay him back immediately, I would either wind up fighting or fucking him.

Dave said, "Seriously man, this is from the Christian locker. God bless you, it sucks here."

Again, I declined his offer, but the other guys in the day room were telling me it was okay. All these motherfuckers were trying to convince me to take the shit from Dave.

Finally, after all of them on my ass, I accepted.

Turns out Dave was a good-ass dude and every time someone new came to our building, he blessed them with supplies. I'd later learn, on the streets, Dave was a crazy meth head who had killed, robbed and hustled people. In prison, however, he was a model citizen.

Two days later, I was headed to the chow hall for lunch, when I looked over in the line next to me and saw my old connect, Angel! I yelled out, "Angel!" and went over to talk to him. At first, he didn't recognize me. It had been over eight years since we'd last seen each other.

After I refreshed his memory, he said, "Didn't you do time for our shit before?" I told him the story of what happened to me. In exchange, he told me his story. He would be in for a long time, since he had gotten caught with several hundred pounds of meth.

Angel was a boss in the drug world and he was a boss on the prison yard. He put the word out I was his long-time homeboy and if anybody fucked with me, they had to deal with him. I had my own guardian Angel in prison.

Building C had a year-long wait to get a two-man cell. It seemed like I was going to be in the day room forever, and I hated the motherfuckers in there. Most of them were troublemakers, which is why they were all jammed together. The day room was where you went when you lost privileges.

Somehow after a month, I got word that one of the best cells in the building was about to come open. I went and pleaded my case with Baker, the building manager and he agreed to put me in the cell. But he also told me I might have to fight for it.

He was wrong. People hated on me for having the good cell and a cool cellmate, but I didn't have to fight. By the time I'd arrived in prison, I weighed 195 pounds and could bench press 325 pounds. I wasn't exactly small like I'd been when I'd gone to state prison.

My new cellmate happened to be from the next city over from where I lived. Turned out, we knew a lot of the same people. I had actually bought meth from him in the past, indirectly. Small world. He had taken out a loan with the company I worked for, too. We instantly got along great.

Federal prison was like a shitty Mexico City hotel with no air conditioning. The Feds know how to help you pass time, though. We had arts and crafts, weight rooms, basketball, handball, movie night and all sorts of other shit to keep us entertained. We even had pay phones we could use 120 minutes per month to call our families.

I'd make a five-minute phone call to W2 each night before bed. One night, she didn't answer. Two days went by with nothing but silence. I was freaking out because I thought she was hurt, in trouble, or God-only-knew.

That Saturday, I was out in the yard playing basketball, when I heard my name called on the intercom for a visit. I wasn't expecting anyone, but I'd take it! When I got to the visiting room, my mom, stepdad and sister were waiting and they had some news.

Apparently, W2 had a boyfriend. The fucking yard boy who mowed my lawn. She had been spotted by my folks kissing dude at the mall. I couldn't believe it. This cunt had set me up from the beginning: she had control of my assets only to spend it on the fucker who was cutting my grass. What a bitch!

I never saw her again. She sent me a letter a month later telling me she had taken all my money, my furniture and my clothes. I'd get out of prison with absolutely nothing. I couldn't understand how she could do that to me. I loved her and she just wanted my shit.

I sunk into an all-time low. Broken, lost, in prison and heartbroken. I just wanted to die. Nine months would fly, but they included a lot of heartache. I had to learn to give up control and accept my life the way it was. The hardest part of prison was what people on the outside were doing to me, not the prisoners.

Chapter 27: Full Release

I'll never forget that day. The day they called me to go home. I was paranoid as fuck because of what had happened to me the first time I had been locked up. But it all worked out; I was out of prison and a free man by noon.

I had a lot to catch up on. Facebook hadn't existed when I went in and Myspace had been the cool thing. While I was locked up, it was like I had been in a cocoon. Many of my friends and past co-workers were jobless and starving. The mortgage world had imploded around me and I had been shut away smoking weed daily in prison.

The mortgage industry, as I knew it, didn't exist anymore. I was not sure what in the hell I would do for work. Most of the mortgage brokers I knew, now had new jobs or had closed shop. No bank would hire a two-time felon either.

With less than $1,200 to my name, a car payment of $600 and two of my tires on my truck rotted, I was broke as fuck. Twenty-eight years old, and living in the home I had sold to my parents just two years before.

Lots of people offered me jobs. Most people knew me as a salesman, so they came flocking to me in droves. I jumped on damn near everything that came my way, but nothing was ever as it was presented to me.

I felt like people were getting over on me and taking advantage of my situation and record. I took opportunity after opportunity that came my way, but none of them ever led to a payday.

Remember that dude who'd worked with me and bailed me out of jail after XW2 had me put in the clink? Yeah, that guy. He had a job at a huge mortgage bank that ran ads on television and that hadn't been affected by the meltdown. It was a solid job he said he could get me.

He had a criminal record, too, so I thought I had a chance. Besides, he was a fucking idiot; if they'd hire him and he'd been able to keep a job, I would be a slam dunk. After hard questioning, I decided to go online and apply. Funny thing was, just two years before, I had been crushing this company and stealing leads from them. Now I was applying to work there.

I had a big chip on my shoulder no one could see. No one knew it, but I was afraid of my own shadow. I'd been fucked over by everyone who loved me. Stolen from, cheated on, imprisoned and more. I knew I could get the job, but in the back of my head, my confidence was gone.

I walked into the interview in clothes that were out of date, but a smile worth a million bucks. One hundred percent real and honest about my past, I showed Rob, my manager, my tax returns. After two hours in his office, we shook hands. I had become an employee of the largest privately held mortgage bank in Texas.

Now, I had a job, but I still needed to get laid like a motherfucker. I'd not had any pussy since 2007 and it was late 2008. Like I said, my confidence was gone and I hadn't had a decent conversation with a woman in almost two years.

With the job in the bag, I needed to celebrate. Even without money to party, I managed to party! When I left the office, I drove up to the bars in the Addison district of Dallas and had a few friends meet me there. They paid for my drinks.

All night they kept saying, "Dawg! Congrats on the job man, but we gotta get you laid!" And shit like that. What they didn't know was that I'd lost my mojo. I was afraid to talk to chicks. My self-worth was zero.

About 11pm, after drinking all day and night, I was at the bar, ready to order my 50th drink or so, when this hot Spanish chick started talking to me. I couldn't hear her name over the music, but I called her Spanish Fly.

She was 41 and looked 25. She took me home and taught me things only a grown-ass woman can teach a man. I must have lasted all of 30 seconds on that first round. Only thing my dick had felt in a long time had been my hand.

Spanish Fly and I went out on a few dates, but she was not girlfriend material. She was fun to hang with and fuck, but not a good match for me personality-wise. Truth be told, I was kind of hung up on XW2.

I was still living at home with my parents and I hadn't officially started my job yet, so each day I would spend my time checking out this site called Facebook. One morning, I got up to go run and I saw I had a notification. It was the girlfriend from 1999, back from when I'd had the OD!

I had been trying to reconnect with her for years and she had ignored my attempts. Then, she hit me up, and I knew what that meant! I immediately responded and worked my way into an agreement to meet up, about to close the longest sales cycle of my life. After all these years, I was still in love with her.

I got her to meet me that Sunday to watch the Cowboys' game. She showed up at my friend's house who had gotten me the job. I said to him, "If you take one look at her and she's fat, tell her wrong person." Because you never know.

When she rang the doorbell, he answered the door and said, "Ryan, it's cool she's hot. I'll let her in." Fucking idiot.

From the moment I re-met her I knew it was on. Before long we were moved in together, too.

Life was finally on track again. I had a good job, a good chick and I was free. Fuck yeah!

Chapter 28: From Top Producer to Bottom Bitch...Again

In September of 2008, I started working as a loan officer for the largest private mortgage bank in Texas. By January, I was a month-over-month, company-wide top producer. I worked my ass off. It was my second chance to get my life and money back together.

The job was high pressure and drove me nuts, but the regular $25,000 paychecks kept me in the grind. Truth is, I loved the job more than I hated it. It just wasn't always rainbows and sunshine.

For book purposes, let's call this bank TXL. TXL is owned by a dude who is worth 30 million cash or more, yet at the time, he drove a 10-year old, piss green trailblazer and his house was falling down. He had to be 35 or older, but he still wore clothes from college. Rich people are weird.

Due to my experiences in prison and working for my dad, I've never been one to schmooze with the higher-ups. In the car wash biz, my stepdad had been the higher-up. I never wanted to hang with him. Matter of fact, I'd avoided him and the managers at all costs.

I'd learned the managers would worry I would replace them, so they'd tell stepdad I smoked, drank, or whatever, in order to keep me under wraps. This made me distant from the chain of command.

In prison, if you are seen talking to a person of authority, such as a lieutenant or warden, you are considered a snitch. For 20+ years, I'd been programed to run like hell from management. Matter of fact, I'd been trained to hate the authority they represented.

That being said, I didn't become top producer by getting choice leads or brown nosing. Upper level management tried to keep me from being number one and couldn't do it. Once they saw my hustle, they couldn't help but respect it.

TXL was a very corporate place. When I first started working there, the team I joined was number two or number three out of four, on a monthly basis. The entire company consisted of about 80 employees, with 30 or so loan officers.

We all worked in a maze of a building. As the company had grown over the years, they had taken more space in this strip mall-type of building. The way to get from one place to another sometimes required passing through a shower room, or going out the back to get in the side door.

While working there I was on parole. I had been sober for almost two years from weed and alcohol. After a month on the job, I got a prescription for Adderall and Xanax. I'd take Adderall in the morning and Xanax before I headed home each night to FW3.

In 2009, I had my systems in place and my business was wide open. TXL was growing despite the fact that most places were shutting their doors. My team had risen to triple-digit monthly closings and we were number one in the company. Thanks to me and a dude I'll call "Nick."

To this day, I still love Nick. He's calmed down a lot now but back then, he was a loose cannon. It was he and I battling each other every month over who would be the number one top producer. Some months, he'd close more volume but I'd do more units, some months, vice versa. It was rare that one of us dominated both categories. We were competitive as hell.

We are also good friends who liked to haze new people and non-producers. Nick can fight, is athletic, sharp and good looking. Needless to say the hate is strong with others towards him. They talk shit like, "He may have made $20K last month, but he still lives at home with his mom." That wasn't true; his mom lived with him.

One day, we were seeing a rather strong influx of leads on phone day and Nick and I ordered pizza for the team. This big, fat bald dude was our boss. He was cool as shit, but was management's boy, not ours. The boss was good about egging us on though.

When the pizza arrived and people went to get a piece, after about 15 minutes, Nick and I decided to cut a hole in this pizza box. He planned to shove his cock in the hole, carry it around dick-in-a-box style and offer the new dudes a slice.

Like I said earlier, you can't kick Nick's ass, so you gotta deal with it. When the first dude opened the box he screamed like a tween girl seeing a dick in real life for the first time. It was hilarious. Nick pulled the prank on two or three others, too. I think the only one who liked it was the processor chick.

As TXL grew, they bought a new building and moved every single team in the company to the new building but us. They wanted to keep the HR threat we were as far away from the rest of the people as possible. They wouldn't fire us because we did too many loans. Half the company's volume came from our team.

The only real problem I had with TXL was their underwriting department. Not only was it slow, they denied shit for no reason. Oh, and the

214

accounting department. They always fucked my checks up. They always fucked everyone's checks up.

About six months in, having become a major player in the company, I decided to stand up for everyone. I wasn't management material, so I fought for the guys who couldn't have a voice. I got the entire sales staff a three percent raise and got us paid twice as fast.

The bean counter's wife hated me for it. She had control over UW, too, so she made my life hell. It was a battle to make these fuckers money each month. I've never seen anything like it. I ended 2009 making over $200K and closing over 160 mortgages. When 2010 rolled around, I had closed 70 loans before March.

Then it came... The Dodd-Frank Act. Once this thing went into play, it kept me from getting a federal license to do my job. My felony meant I couldn't get a license to write loans.

TXL could have fought for me, but they hated me because I fought for the salesmen not the company. So even though I asked for them to get a lawyer and help me, they denied my request. The CEO was shifty, he would rather lose me, who earned them $40K+ each month (just their cut), than help me out.

Shit ruined my brain worse than prison. Here was another person I had done good work for who'd turned their back on me. Without a broker going to battle for me, hiring my own lawyer was useless. TXL simply didn't want their name mixed up with mine. They were okay with me making them cash, but when shit got tough, just like everyone else had done in my life, they bolted.

When was this shit gonna end? I would find out, not anytime soon.

Chapter 29: Shitweasel City

If I thought the fake recruiters were bad when I got out of prison, I had no clue how bad they would be when they found out I was unemployed. Allow me to explain...

Remember the dude who got me the job at TXL? He had been fired for stealing and had a new job at a title company. The title company rented out space to a small three-man broker shop.

The CEO of that broker shop (let's call him Knob) and the lending company, Blueballs Lending, arranged a meeting with me. I was still pissed at the mortgage industry as a whole and I wasn't even sure if that was what I was going to do with the rest of my life anymore.

Sure, I was conflicted as hell, but I took the meeting with Knob anyway. When we met, Knob was impressed with my numbers and made me an offer I couldn't refuse. He said he'd let me be the marketing rep and he would do all the loans. All I had to do was send him the names and numbers of the leads.

It seemed like a dream come true! My only responsibility was to make the sale, then this fool would do the paperwork. What LO wouldn't dream of this? He also offered to pay me a $30K salary and a sliding scale bonus based off lead volume.

So, I went to work.

A few days in, I created a Facebook page for Blueballs and started running ads to it. This was back in 2010, so it was brand new territory in the lending world. Instead of me trying to sell them on the phone, I figured I'd just send prospects to the online application and direct the apps over to Knob. If it worked, I would have effectively replaced myself with technology and I would still get paid.

Guess what? It worked! Applications started coming in and for $10/day, we were getting leads every day. After that, I took my email skills and started mailing my list of past clients and referral partners.

I made an email follow-up sequence and sent it manually each day of the week. From that alone, I started getting 510 apps per week. Next thing you know, the CEO is buried in paperwork and I'm smoking weed leaving the office at 10 in the morning!

Guess who got jealous as fuck? Yeah, that cunt, Knob. I'll never forget what that fucker did to me. It was four days after my birthday, and he fired me for making a video, took my commissions and when I threatened to report him, had me sign a 12-month gag order so he could get 20 percent of the cash he owed me.

He basically took my pipeline, stole my commissions and silenced me at Christmas. For two months he'd said, "I'll get you paid man." But come Christmas time, I was broke. I couldn't afford to give W3 a gift and we were busted. I still hate that fucker. He did it to a few of my other friends who left TXL to work there, too. Rat bastard.

At the same time, I had been attending a church we'll call CCC, in the suburbs. I had started at this church when it had been situated in an elementary school, and watched it grow into a $3.5 million expansion building "for the glory of God."

When I'd first gotten out of prison in 2008, the church leaders had reserved me a spot in some MLM thing. This church was all about MLM. Any way they could sell you something, they would.

When Knob fucked me, the church crew showed me how I had a big down line already, thanks to them. If I just worked a little, I'd make fast money. I was stupid enough to believe that it was a sign from God, so I went all-in.

I put my self-taught, online marketing skills to work and I started recruiting people through

Facebook and SEO. I quickly worked up the pin ranks and made a few thousand dollars a month. After a number of months of really getting good at the recruiting game, I looked up to see the company had changed the comp plan and product on me. I lost it all. My down line. My income. My confidence.

FUCK!

I was at an all-time business low, so I reached out to my pal, Mike. Mike and I had traded referrals when he'd been a realtor. He was still an agent at the time, but most of his money had come from online sales of some sort.

At lunch that day, he told me about his business and I thought he was speaking Greek. He took me back to his office and gave me some CD-ROMs to watch from a dude whose hometown was also Austin. The CDs were about continuity. *WTF was that?*

I checked out the CDs and quickly called Mike to ask him to meet me to watch the UFC fight. During the fight, Mike kept on about how he'd just been on a private plane with some guru surfer out of La Jolla, and he kept insisting that I watch these specific videos. He told me, "You have to watch this shit man, you have to."

The next day, I woke up and immediately Googled what Mike told me to. My life was about to change, but more shit weasels had to make their run on me first.

After learning what Mike was up to, I wanted to be just like him. I met him for breakfast once a week at his live mastermind. Everyone at breakfast worked with him, but me. I was just there to take it all in.

One of the dudes on his team was familiar from the past. Turned out, he used to try and sell me credit repair, but he had started selling for Mike. I got to know the guy; he went to the CCC church and we seemed to get along.

I tried to do a few business deals with him, but he wasn't much of an action taker. One day though, he brought this dude to breakfast when Mike wasn't there, who supposedly had sold $150 million in real estate in the last year.

In the Dallas market, that was an absurd amount of business. He was crazy as shit, gay as could be and didn't give a shit about what others thought of him. I wanted to know how this guy had sold so much real estate looking like a bum. Literally, he resembled the Big Lebowski.

After a few talks and some ideas floating around, the dude and I decided to start one of the very first social media management services for agents. He used his track record in sales, my marketing skills and W3's writing skills to leverage the shit out of it.

Somehow, from his gay, Chinese, teenage-looking boyfriend, he even got a $50,000 loan. I was all about putting the $50K into marketing and rolling this bad boy out. Dude wanted to let another partner in, we'll call him Lazy Sanchez, and for us to spend the money on an event in San Francisco. We'd also take $10K each in cash up front.

With all the promises flying around, how could I lose? I took the $10K, went to San Francisco only to find out everything we thought was set up, wasn't. Sanchez took his money and ran, bought a car and was never heard from again. The Lebowski Dude opened up a bank account, charged a bunch without authorization and left the tab in the company name we had set up.

All this shit happened in roughly four months. I had personally worked my ass off (again) and gotten us around 70 clients who'd paid an average of $700 each, to let us write Facebook posts for them.

One day, after arguing with the dude for over an hour, I realized I was doing all the work; he couldn't match talent and I was splitting money for nothing.

I sent in my letter of resignation to share forfeiture and quit.

I was tired of working with partners. I was now in a space where I was sick of relying on other people. I was battered from getting fucked over. A lot of people think they can keep up with me, but when they see the machine at work, they can't.

Too bad it took me 30 years to learn it. I swear to everything I have; I've never done anything in my life the easy way. No shortcuts, no corner cuts, nothing. I wish I could lie and cheat like other people. But I have always been the patsy. Maybe I wasn't as smart as I thought.

I wasn't smart, I'd been a fucking idiot. But I knew I was still an action taker. I'll take action over intelligence any day when it's all I got.

Chapter 30: A Car Salesman on a Mission

During the shitweasel business phase I was going through, some life changes happened. I'd officially been broke as fuck and on my last leg of life in December of 2010.

In 2009, I married W3. She was the same chick from 1999 who'd left me, which led to me eventually OD'ing on coke.

It wasn't her fault. I'm just reestablishing a timeline here.

Anyways, I was flat broke, had run through our entire savings; she was a housewife due to me telling her it was okay to quit her job when I'd been making $25,000 a month, and shit was fucked.

To make matters worse, W3 was not used to this roller coaster ride bullshit I had her on. She's very delicate and not a street-tough thug like me. She grew up with money in a good family home. I was attracted to her due to the fact she was nothing like me, or any previous chicks I'd been with.

In January of 2011, she hadn't had her period, so we went to the doctor. She was prego! I was going to be a dad. It was a game changer in my life. She, of course worried if she would be able to keep "it" long enough to give birth, but I knew it was our time.

I'd like to tell you "nine months later," there was Jax," but that's not how it happened. I was flat busted, remember? I was an entrepreneur, remember? I had no insurance; she had no job and we were broke as fuck.

I remember smoking weed one morning in my home office, thinking I had only nine months to get my shit together. I was destitute, jobless and had no foreseeable income. We had to borrow some cash from her folks. It was our only choice.

I decided I needed to get a real job that provided insurance just in case something went wrong with Jax's birth. So, I called a friend I'd met from prison who was a manager at a car dealership and told him my situation. He told me to come in, but said I'd have to take a drug test. So I asked him to gimme 48 hours.

Weed stays in most people's systems for about 30 days. For me, it's about 30 hours. I don't know why, but THC processes through my body quickly. I'd learned this from being on parole and smoking and taking drug tests. Forty-eight hours later, I passed the test and got the job.

I was a fucking car salesman and I worked that Texas summer in the 103-degree heat showing black on black F150s like they were going out of production. I bet I walked 10 miles every day across that parking lot.

Still, I quickly showed my sales skills and rose to the top of the force, but I never got to the number one spot because I ONLY worked the required hours. I wanted to be home any chance I could to help W3.

Also while I was there, I was able to test out some of my video and social media ideas. The dealership had a good flow of leads coming in. Each day for the first couple months, I'd go and make a video.

The other salesmen made fun of me and laughed at my antics, but I outsold all except one each month. The customers loved it and I knew if I could get people to love me as a car salesman, I could sell anything via video online.

In May of 2010, I started a blogtalk radio show called *Sales Finesse*. I'd go out to my car each Thursday at 1pm and record the show live over my cell phone. I'd tell people I had a radio show, but all it was, was me talking into the phone about sales for an hour each week.

Nobody listened to those shows. I was just recording my thoughts into thin air and no one cared. Didn't matter to me though; I treated every episode like a million people were listening. Eventually, they did. Well, not a million, but over 100 thousand!

Again, the car guys laughed at me, but I was on a mission. I didn't even realize I had been doing what's called a podcast, the whole time. Turned out my shit was on iTunes. Nobody was listening to it, but I was proud because I was leaving a legacy for Jax.

I'd leave early, duck out and disappear, anything I could do to get away from that dealership. Yes, I wanted to make money and work up the chain to ownership, but that also seemed like a lot of work and I wasn't good at brown nosing.

Chapter 31: It's Jax!

September came around and I knew any day now, W3 was going to pop. I was already a father, but it was soon going to be time for me to be a dad. As you know, I hadn't had the best examples of parents, so I just knew I was going to be awesome.

When I was in federal prison, I wrote some guidelines for how I wanted to raise my son. I was about to put those plans into action. I'll never forget the day as long as I'm alive.

I was nervous as hell. I'm OCD and was worried about my hands getting blood all over them. I don't like the sight of that kind of stuff, so I didn't want to watch the birth. I didn't want to ruin my perception of the vagina.

I stayed in that room, weed-free all day waiting on Jax to show up. I had no idea what I was going to do when he did, though. When the time came, and he was born, I grabbed him from the doctor and immediately cried. My baby boy was here!

After a few days in the hospital, we were able to leave. I took extra special care of the car seat detail. Prior to Jax's birth, I had taken three parenting classes. I'm coachable, so I wanted to learn CPR and other useful stuff I should know as a parent.

When we got him home, I felt as if my life was going to be okay for once. If nothing else, I would always have Jax on my side. As long as I didn't push him away like my folks had done to me.

I was lucky as hell. Jax didn't cry too much. He was easy to take care of and W3 is a great mom. She has like 19 nieces and nephews and her dad worked for a children's hospital. She had a shitload of shit-changing experience.

It sucked for me. I'd go to work all day, stick to my routine of working out at 5am, work at 8am and then off work at 9pm. Very rough. I missed my son and wanted to be at home with him 24/7. I was trying to find a way out.

Thanksgiving rolled around and the dealership wouldn't give me an extra day off, so I just quit. I was tired, bored and wanted more for my son. I had been offered a job at a title company and I was going to take it. Win or not, it couldn't get any worse.

After a month of no income, I was forced to borrow money from W3's family again. She had no job, wouldn't get a job and I was still trying to find my way. To make matters worse, W3 wanted to get out of the house we were in. She said it was bad stigma for her.

So, there I was, borrowing money from my in-laws, searching for a renter of my current home, looking to rent a new home and without a job. Seems legit! Not to mention my beautiful baby boy (triple B) who's got an old man he needs to look up to and not be ashamed of; I had to get my shit together.

In all honesty, W3 had no idea if we had cash or not. She just did her thing. She wanted a new home and I was going to make it happen. I found a home to rent in the neighborhood we wanted. I also found a renter for our home.

Everything was in place to make the move and the renters were in my home when the people who were going to rent to me changed their mind about my felony. Last minute, too. I was now officially homeless. I had taken the much needed rent and down payment from my renters and paid my bills. Again, I had no choice, but to beg my in-laws to let us move in with them.

Six months after Jax was born, I was living with my in-laws and barely had an income. My mom and stepdad thought I was scamming people, and one day my mom called to chew my ass. I'd had enough.

All my life, my stepdad and mom had put me through hell. Beatings, hard labor, steroids, guns, running away and everything in-between. I decided after that call I wanted nothing more to do with my family. I wanted to be free. I was sick of hiding their shit and making it my shit.

I also didn't want them around Jax because I wanted him raised according to my plan and they were no longer a part of it. It was like a million-pound weight had been lifted off my shoulders. It's amazing what you will do for your kids that you won't do for yourself.

Doesn't change the fact I had become a broke, barely employed, living-with-in-laws dad, who kept failing at life. Dammit, I had to get my shit together for my son. It was eating me up inside. How the hell had I kept hitting rock bottom and so many times? Was I never going to get this thing called life down?

My worst fear was that if I'd died right then, my son would only know me as a loser with no legacy to be proud of. Other than my podcast, I had nothing to leave him. I was fucking embarrassed.

All I wanted to do was be the dad I'd never had. It was time to take massive action in order to make it happen. This title company that had just given me a job didn't know what was about to hit them.

I was about to do it big and all for Jax. Tired of being broke and a joke; people looked up to me and I was failing. I had to turn this ship around. Without a minute to spare and for my baby boy. He didn't deserve this life. I wanted to literally spoil him.

Chapter 32: The Birth of Hardcore Closer

On Thanksgiving of 2011, I finally had a day off from selling cars. When Friday rolled around, I wanted to stay home with Jax. I had spent all day with him on turkey day and didn't want to leave him.

I called into the dealership and quit. The prior week I had met with the guy who owned a title company. He wanted me to sell title insurance for him and market his brand, told me I could make $20-30K a month, just like I'd done in mortgages. The catch that I wouldn't find out until the day I started, was that I was commission-only with no leads.

I had to make my own way, my own contacts and close my own sales. Why was I going to build this guy's business for free? When the smoke clears, the sales pitch is never what the result reflects.

When I was a LO, I hated title companies. After a few days working there and realizing all LOs felt the same way I did, I knew I was going to have to do something way outside of the box.

Since 2009, I had been learning how to do lots of things online. I'd had success with video and email sales while I'd been in the car business, now I was going to get a chance to try it in the real estate industry. Each night when I got home, I would spend 1-3 hours learning new stuff. I was a sponge with nothing better to do.

I lived with my in-laws and although Jax and W3 hung out with them downstairs quite a bit, I felt like a loser and mostly hid upstairs behind my computer. I would watch any kind of marketing training I could. I wanted to learn it all.

One day, my sister went to work for a mortgage company as a LO assistant. She reached out to me to help her boss with marketing. I talked to him, recited my fees and told him what I could do. He seemed interested, but I didn't close him. It was 2012, social media hadn't caught on and was nothing like it is today.

About an hour after I got off the phone with him, my mom called me. She was complaining about me trying to take money from my little sister and how I was breaking the law by getting paid for marketing. I snapped.

I'd taken on debt for my folks, helped them sell houses, buy cars and I'd even run guns and steroids for my stepdad, who had no regard for my personal safety. I was a grown-ass man who was suddenly tired of hiding my stories of prison, adoption and everything else.

I told her I didn't ever want her or my stepdad to see W3, Jax, or me again. They weren't doing anything but holding me back. I felt imprisoned by their lies and I wanted to clear my conscience.

I made a decision that day I still haven't changed my mind on—I had to let my family go. Being around them always caused a lot of painful memories. And when we would all party and drink together on holidays, it seemed like something always went down. It was exhausting.

Once it was said and over with, I felt like Atlas dropping the world. Yeah, it shook and hurt a little, but it had to be done or it would eventually kill me. I had to protect Jax from the abuse and I was totally fine having W3, Jax and my in-laws as my only family. When I cross a bridge, I usually burn it to the ground, then dynamite it just to make sure it's dead.

I went to work at the title company that next Monday and talked to the dude who'd gotten me the job. It was the same dude who'd also placed me at TXL. I told him about my folks and what happened. He knew me and he knew them and simply said, "That's hardcore."

Right then, it dawned on me! I went into my office, shut the door and registered the domain www.hardcorecloser.com. Within the next three hours, I had a blog up and several videos uploaded. I was on my way to being the first dude to help LOs close more loans through the usage of the interwebs. I was gonna be rich...or was I?

Oh I forgot, I never get a lucky break! Fuck me!

In 2012, people didn't want to hear how Facebook could get business for them. Especially large companies who had the website blocked from their servers. The people I convinced to let me help, all had to get special permission just to access the site. This was before the app functioned the way it does now on our phones.

Managers would hang up on me. LOs would tell me it was irrelevant to them and they didn't need it. They would say social media is a waste of time and laughed at the fact I called myself a social media consultant. It wasn't like it is these days.

Nevertheless, I stuck to it. I never got that much title business though. It just never took off for me. The title company owner even hooked me up with his Internet buddies who had this QR code software for agents.

I helped these guys sell over 3,000 subscriptions of their service in 48 hours by putting a one-minute sales pitch out to over 5,000 agents. I'd tell 5-10 agents the same pitch all at once to make the most of my time.

I remember day three at that job. I'd gone to take a piss first thing upon arriving at the convention center. When I went into the bathroom, I saw a bag of coke on the floor and picked it up. After I finished pissing, I took it to them and was jokingly like, "Look what I found. Realtors know how to party, huh?"

I guess they thought it was my coke and not funny at all. They didn't have the balls to say anything to my face, but when we got on the plane back, it was evident something wasn't right. After we deplaned, I never heard from them again.

I ended up having to sue them to get my expenses and commissions back. I had to give half my earnings to an attorney, so the whole trip was nothing more than a learning lesson. A lesson on what was possible. A lesson that agents were grasping technology and LOs were falling behind.

My mission as a "Hardcore Closer" was clear: to teach number-crunching LOs how to use technology to market. I never intended on taking the name "Hardcore Closer" for myself. After a while though, people just started calling me "Closer" and it stuck. Not a bad name to have actually, now that I think about it.

I was still broke, though. The only thing hardcore about my life at that time was Hardcore poverty. Hardcore idiot was more like it. I didn't quit; I knew I was onto something, I just had to endure the power to ride it out until I struck oil.

I started filming local LOs with my own camera. I would script out things to say and teach them how to put their sales pitches and FAQ on autopilot so they could go out and prospect more. It was funny to watch these guys who were 50+ years old get on camera and freeze. I'd show them what to do, but it wasn't natural for them.

Since they didn't like how they looked on video, they wouldn't use the videos and since they didn't use them, they sure didn't see any results. It was a bad cycle for business. Next, I tried to teach them how to post to get people to like them and do business with them on Facebook.

Again, no one took action. Here it was, wide open prospecting and no one was interested in taking advantage of it. I've always been amazed by the amount of people who simply, just won't take action. Sometimes a little action makes a huge difference.

So, I took action for them and started charging a $500 setup fee and $100 monthly recurring fee to write and post for them on Facebook. I worked my ass off, sold a bunch of spots, fucked off two business partners and made a lot of LOs and agents money.

I personally wrote five posts a day for about 70 people, which gave me fast action and an inside look at the way different social media audiences responded to different posts. I'd have the clients take a personality type test when they signed up that asked religious, political, work and family-related questions. From there, I could get them friends and prospects.

I got good at it until one day, when I became fed up with all the stress of writing and I shut it down. Actually, *I* shut down, resigned and sold my shares over to one of the business partners.

I had experience and a game plan now. It was time to get what was coming to me.

Chapter 33: The Level Up

It was January 2013, when I got a message on Facebook from a past mentor. I've always been about having a mentor, but hadn't ever really paid anyone to mentor me. I'd go to lunch or get on the phone with people I looked up to, but I had never paid someone for advice on business and life.

They say good advertising should seem like a sign from God. "Oh this is exactly what I needed right now," should be the expression people have when they see your offers. I was in a period of my life I needed to escape, but wasn't sure how.

I felt trapped. My business partner was way too intertwined in all of my dealings and as usual, wasn't carrying his weight. I was at a breaking point when I got the message.

"Hey man, I'm not sure if you know or not, but I'm trying to help a couple of dudes like you make six-figures a month.

You interested?"

He didn't have to sell me. I knew I needed someone with more experience than me to teach me how to break out of my bullshit situation.

Within a matter of minutes, I had committed to the biggest financial investment I had ever made in a year. It cost more than 99 percent of the cars on the road. Was it worth it?

I'm writing this book ain't I?

The first conversation I had with my new mentor was about what I wanted to do in life. I was managing social media accounts for small business owners and it was catching up to me. Posting for around 70 people, on five networks, five times a day, meant I was writing my ass off.

After about an hour or so on the phone, I wasn't clear about what I wanted to do, but I was clear that I didn't want to do this anymore. Once that was settled, I had to find out two more things: (1) what I was going to do for money and (2) how could I escape the leech biz partner?

As bad as I wanted to stop writing, the leech wanted to keep it going. It was looking like I had the perfect situation. I could quit, hand over my shares and let him keep the money and clientele. Later on, if something happened, I could put the responsibility on him.

Within a few days, I had every detail planned out on paper. All I had to do was to put my plan into action. Funny thing about action, it makes most people uncomfortable, so they don't take it. I like being out of my comfort zone, and I'm pretty easy to get riled up. I went straight for the jugular with brutal honesty about how I hated my role in the company and wanted out.

Just as I suspected, he wanted to pick up the slack, aka money, where I'd left off. So, as I resigned and forked over my shares, he got ready to take over the whole company and turn it into a million-dollar venture.

But…he ran it into the ground in less than a month.

On that first 1.5-hour phone call, my mentor asked me why I had such a dumb-ass as a partner. I started thinking about it, and turned out I'd had a long trail of dumb-asses as partners. From Brant to the Leech. It was time for me to do something about it. What the fuck was I doing with my life? I was over this struggle, for real.

I still had the problem of not knowing what in the fuck I was going to do for money. I remember saying, "There are dry cleaners on every corner around here, maybe I should market for them." I just wanted to make money and get out of my in-laws' house.

The second phone call, we focused on what I was going to do for money. *With my expertise in mortgage and real estate, why was I not working with those industries?* I had been bitter as fuck about losing my ability to originate, but this could be my way back into a business I loved.

More importantly, if I started working with agents first, the LOs would come flocking to me to find out how I'd gotten all these agents in my network. So, I went to work.

Within about three days of that second phone call, I made a $2,500 sale to Sean Matheis. He and I had met a few weeks before and he had the hook up with agents and wanted to sell more insurance to LO's clients.

I actually sold him by accident when I called him to see which agent he knew who might be interested in the offer. He paused and said, "Fuck the agents, I'll do it." This worked out even better for me, because I knew Sean was an action taker.

Within a month of working with me, his production had more than quadrupled. He was writing 100+ policies a week for the insurance company, by himself. This opened my eyes up to what was possible. Like any good shark, the taste of blood (a sale) only made me want to make more.

After a month, I was running full steam and using Facebook and YouTube to market the shit out of myself. Every day all day, I'd message people on Facebook asking if they could use my help. The same as my mentor had done with me.

I'm a fast action taker, so it wasn't long before I had run out of friends to hit up. I had to figure something out and quickly because I needed leads. People who knew me wouldn't give me a chance; I had to get in front of judgmental-free strangers.

I needed to figured out how to run ads. It would be the only way I would be able to stay in the game. I knew how to sell and market; next, I needed to know how to advertise.

My mentor invited me to come to his house in Las Vegas in May of 2013. It was a trip and event I will never forget. When I arrived at his house, the people I had been following for three years online were all there. This guy had famous clients and I was now one, too. Although not famous (yet), I felt like I was in a place with my peers.

In that house, I was taught how to run Facebook ads by a British dude, who was from Ohio and who, at that time, resided in California. He also happened to be the world record holder for the strongest man on the planet. He showed me how to make a simple lead funnel that could be boosted through Facebook.

We set it all up and went off to lunch at the Anthem Country Club. By the time we got back, I had over 40 leads. Game on!

As expected, I started closing clients into my mastermind that day. I'd flown to LV flat-ass busted, and left with about $25,000 in new earnings. I had finally broken through!

I didn't stop there and just stick with the plan, though. I invested another $100,000 of money that year into other masterminds. From Facebook experts to SEO, I paid for it all. I now knew how to get leads and close them. I'd absorbed how to officially turn air into money.

Chapter 34: Return of the Closer!

You know, I'd like to sit here and tell you it's been all uphill since that fateful day in Las Vegas. But if I did that, I'd be a fucking liar and the whole purpose of this entire book would be lost. Instead, in the tradition of this book and my life, I'm going to keep it real with you.

It was now mid-2013, and I was making decent cash again, earning around $25,000 gross each month, which was a long way up from the $2,500 I had been earning for the last few years. Every time I hit a lick, something had always shown up to take it.

I wasn't living life the way I wanted to yet. I was still carrying all the secrets you've read throughout this book. And I couldn't get where I wanted to go by holding back on who I was. I didn't want to make an announcement or anything like that, I just knew I couldn't lie or cover up anything anymore.

Around July 2013, I was invited to be a guest on a podcast by a fellow member of one of the masterminds I'd been a part of. On that podcast, the host asked me to "tell a little bit about myself" and I don't think I took a breath for 45 minutes. It felt like a 10-ton brick had been lifted off my back. I had finally set my burdens free.

Well, that pissed a lot of people off. I lost family, friends and eventually W3. I had to learn, once I got comfortable with myself, what I really wanted in life. That meant I also had to get clear on what I didn't want.

To this day, I've lost a wife, parents, grandparents and other close friends and family due to this story. It seems as if I'm the source of everyone's shame. Sure, they like it when I'm successful, but they'd rather live in darkness, where I'd rather live in truth.

Once I adopted this mindset, my consulting business exploded. In a good way! When I got started, I offered free strategy sessions to anyone who wanted one. I'd get a shit ton of leads, but very few of them could afford me. I call them the Freeple.

Once I was super confident and comfortable in my own skin, I changed my sales pitch from free strategy sessions to a new message: only contact me if you have money and are serious. The definition of serious is in the eye of the beholder, but it definitely has helped keep a steady flow of clients coming my way each month.

Remember Sean? The first person to hit me up and become a client? Yeah, that guy went on to become a master networker and he has connected me to multiple celebrities. He was the one example I could always point to.

In late 2013, Sean and I started Millionaire Masterminds and quickly recruited Josh Flagg, Fredrik Eklund, Katrina Campins and Craig Robertson to lead training courses alongside us. I personally wrote a pitch for Dan Bilzerian that was accepted until the brokers, lawyers and agents got involved. By the time everyone got paid, there was none left for me. I'm not a charity.

Sean and I joke about our work on Million Dollar Listing. We ran campaigns on social media for up to $750 per day for almost an entire month. We sold a quarter of a million dollars in mastermind dues during that time. We added tens of thousands of fans on Facebook and the following season they were nominated for an Emmy. This was way before the networks knew about FB ads, when their biggest marketing medium was advertising on taxi cabs.

I literally went from adoption, prison, divorce and homelessness to making cameos on national TV shows and being on some of the most popular podcasts on iTunes. At one time, people decided to make a reality show about me. We filmed it in Arizona, but I didn't like the way they wanted the show to be, so I dropped it.

The TV show gig happened after my divorce in 2014. Even though I wasn't a fan of the desert, I went to Arizona every weekend for three months straight. While I was there, I met Amy. I didn't like Arizona, but I believe there's a reason for everything.

Amy lived in Scottsdale and is a stockbroker. She's also fine as fuck. Not only is she a closer, my female counterpart, but she's also a great person, mother and girlfriend. She and her son, Asher moved to Texas for work and to be closer to me at the end of 2014.

Writing this book and reflecting on where I've come from and where I am at now, makes me tear up. I'm putting this all down from one of the most exclusive high rise buildings in Dallas. I've got a beautiful son, a smoking hot girl and an Asher! When I go pick up Asher from school, I have to drive through the hood to get there—the same hood where
I fired that shot on the longest day. I still find it hard to believe I made it out.

I'm proof that you can, too. All you have to do is want it bad enough. You have to make the decision that no matter how hard times get you won't go back to crime. Notice how I never went back to selling drugs or breaking the law? I made a promise to myself that I kept, even after the second time I went to prison for no reason.

I write this book for you, the person who wants to be a renegade, but thinks you have to break the law to do so. You can be your own person. You can live life on your terms. You just have to do so with morals and within the law.

I have encountered every excuse there is to fail, and I have failed thousands of times. The difference, I did not accept failure. I got back up, fought and refused to relent. If you, too, adopt this mindset, it will serve you, and those around you, for life.

AFTERWARD

I woke up this morning in one of the most expensive buildings in Dallas, next to the hottest blonde I've ever seen. Last week, I was in Tampa. This week, I head to Pensacola Beach. The best part is that my family gets to join me.

Last September, I met Amy, my perfect brain twinsie. She has a son, Asher, who is a year younger than Jax. They are BFF's. The four of us live on the 15th floor of a high rise.

My business is hitting six-figures a month in gross income, and I'm ONLY working on the things I like working on and ONLY doing business with the people I like.

My blog, www.hardcorecloser.com is getting over 400,000 visitors a month and I couldn't ask for a better life. I'm actually thinking about leasing a Ferrari.

All of this is proof anything is possible. Two prison sentences, three divorces and one hell of a life. My goal is for you to feel encouraged to go out and do the same with your life. To overcome. It's never too late to win.

Made in the USA
Middletown, DE
13 December 2018